The Beautiful Crafts Book

STERLING
PUBLISHING CO., INC.
NEW YORK

Published in the United States of America by
Sterling Publishing Co., Inc., 419 Park Avenue South,
New York, N.Y. 10016
Published in Canada by Saunders of Toronto, Ltd.

First published in USA in 1976
Third impression 1978
Copyright © 1976 Search Press Limited London/
Christophorus Verlag Freiburg im Breisgau, Federal
Germany

ISBN 0-8069-5366-7 Trade
      0-8069-5367-5 Library

Phototypeset by Tradespools Ltd, Frome, Somerset
Made and printed in Spain

The Beautiful Crafts Book

Contents

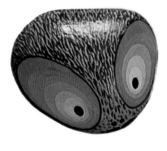

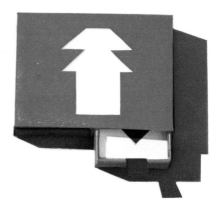

Wooden toys Page 65
Animals for children. Funny figures for birthdays. Wooden toys are still the best and give the longest-lasting delight.

Fabric printing Page 82
You can turn out a vast number of single-color materials in simple as well as highly decorative designs by making your own stencils.

Match-box games Page 108
An entire game in a match-box. Just the thing for school-children and for adults with a cheerful spirit.

Painting old furniture Page 70
Don't throw that old kitchen chair away. It can cheer up the room or even become a valuable art-work in its own right.

Lino-cutting Page 88
From simple engraving on linoleum blocks to four-color work requiring more precision – here are the basics of this ever-popular modern craft.

Wall decorations Page 116
Original works of art are expensive these days. Why not make your own wall sculptures and decorations and enrich your rooms and club or school.

Batik on wood and paper Page 76
Most people think of batik work as applied to fabrics, but it's amazing what results you can achieve on ordinary wood and paper.

Easter eggs Page 96
You don't have to make these rich and beautiful objects at Easter; they are marvellous presents all the year round.

Painting stones

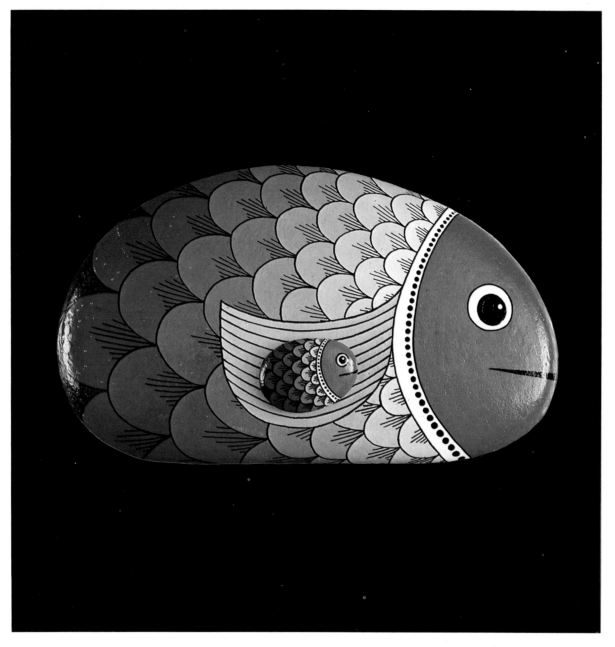

You can find the raw materials for stone painting when you're out for a country walk or strolling along the beach. Paths, ditches, banks of streams and rivers, fields, forest clearings, even building-sites, gardens (and yards) can yield the most surprising treasures for stone decorators. Once the enthusiasm has really gripped you, you won't be able to resist stones whenever you see them, in all their shapes and sizes. Some of your finds will show you how polluted the streams of our world are. It will take more than one scrubbing with a strong detergent to remove the green algae that adhere to the river specimens.

Of course, you will sometimes find "special" stones so exceptional that it would be quite wrong to paint them. You will already have enjoyed one of the pleasures of stonecraft in discovering a form which you can appreciate as a unique miniature sculpture. You don't need to "ruin" it: there are plenty of other less finished pieces waiting for the complement of your own creativity.

But have you ever looked closely at stones?

The illustrations in this chapter are intended to stimulate your own ideas. You don't have to copy them exactly. You can get much more fun out of painting stones if you develop your own first impressions.

Perhaps you've always thought that they were all like one another: uniformly, boringly gray. All you need do to rid yourself of this idea is to make a stone-hunting expedition on a rainy day. If you look down on stony ground and concentrate for a moment, you'll be astonished to see pebbles in their glory for the first time. They have many hues; they shimmer and shine; they are streaked and loaded with rich ore; some are small-scale architectural masterpieces. If you want to preserve this kind of rainwashed glory for an appreciable time, then paint your best finds with a clear varnish or lacquer, or work on them with a fine white wax polish.

You'll often happen upon a stone which says quite unmistakably at the first glance that it's a fish or a porcupine, a mouse or a cat, or any one of the multitudinous forms nature has bestowed upon the paradise of stones as well as the kingdom of animals. Sometimes the unique shape you pick out will be a symbolic form: a heart, for instance.

You now have a small stock of stones. Of

course you have to wash them before getting down to work, not just out of general cleanliness but because your final coat of paint will come out better on the natural tone and texture of pebbles and rocks.

It's best to use poster paints. They dry quickly. How many jars you start out with depends on your taste and pocket. You can do a lot with only a jar of black and one of white: some stunning *art nouveau* or even mod pop designs are possible with black, white and gray. Or you can choose something like yellow and red – a combination allowing a range of intermediate shades. Primaries are obvious choices; yellow and blue giving green, and so on. Stone painting needn't be expensive.

Then all you need is a few brushes: a strong, thick one (Nos. 4–6) for the ground color or for large areas, and then one or two fine brushes (Nos. 0–1) for decoration and finishing. These fine brushes must be of the best quality material you can get; otherwise you won't get the precise detail that builds

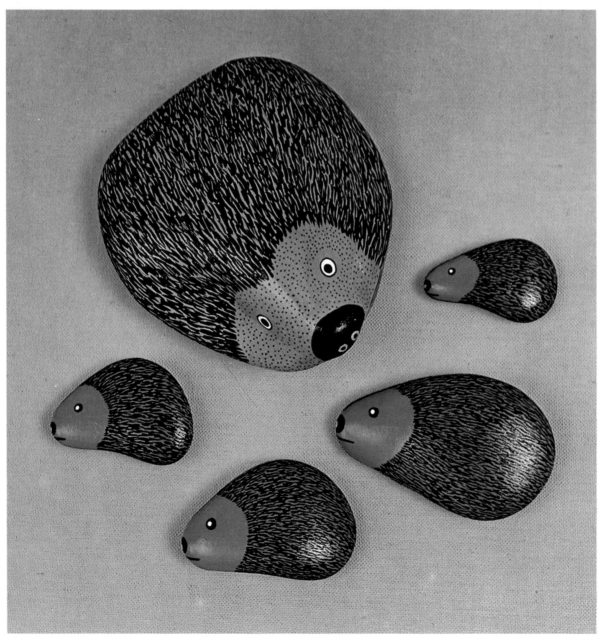

If you're lucky enough to discover two stones of exactly the same shape, you can use them as twins. If they are of different sizes, then you have a mother-and-child pair. A whole family can be built up in this way.

Hedgehogs and porcupines are very easily reproduced. If the stones are light enough (you can see that under running water) paint the spines straight on. Otherwise, use a light ground.

up to the effect achieved in the picture opposite. Try a brush to see if it gives a perfect dot or a minute tinted circle; then you'll know how good or bad it is.

Don't forget to work on sheets of clean newspaper. You need a bowl of water for thinning out the poster paints and another for rinsing out the brushes when changing colors.

Select the stone that you find most attractive. Find out whether it has a light or dark base color, and a smooth or rough

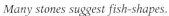

Many stones suggest fish-shapes.

surface (on the dominant side). Are there any unevennesses, holes, sudden bumps, or other irregularities? Which side is best? Can it be made to stand on end? All these points are important. Any one of them can suggest a new avenue of design or a telling detail.

Are you going to paint the entire surface of the specimen? Sometimes that is advisable. Usually, when the stone is covered with scratches but has a generally interesting outline, you will be reluctant to throw it away. But perhaps all you need to do is to paint a few spots here and there.

Most people leave the lower half of the stone or under-surface (on which it lies and which no one ever really catches sight of) as it is. Then they have only half as much work to do.

You can trace your rough design on the stone in soft pencil. You can scratch it in if necessary. If you like the overall conception after that, then all you have to do is to fill in the main color areas on the broad surface of the stone.

It often makes the work easier if you put a book of the same thickness as the stone you're working on next to it, and use it as a support for your hand.

If you want to produce fish shapes, many variations are offered by scales. You can do

A natural shape like this just has to be turned into a cat. (The white ring on the round stone was there from the start, but the head could be brought out more with a thicker border.)

big and small, elongated or broad-thick, rainbow stripes, or only partly-painted scales.

The paint shouldn't be too thin and shouldn't run, but on the other hand you'll be in trouble if you smear it on too thickly.

If you're working with exceptionally light colors, such as white, yellow or orange, and if the stone is dark, it doesn't help at all to make the paint thicker. You have to let the first coat dry and then apply a second one. Or you can give the stone a white ground to

start with and then make sure that the top colors come out well. Don't use more than three coats.

If you want to be more exact in demarcating the individual colors on the painted stone, make the edges of each color area sharper; or if you just like doodling, you need a mapping pen or its equivalent and some India or China ink (preferably one made for use with a fountain-pen), which is best for drawing on the dry poster paint. The stone needs a final

13

coating of protective lacquer or varnish. Some colors run – especially blue and purple, usually when they're next to white. In these cases you'll have to use a more expensive spray lacquer. Only varnish one half of the stone at a time. Varnishes can take from two hours to a day to dry. Consult your art supplies or crafts shop on the properties of the varnish when used with poster paints.

You can use the stone as if it were a sheet of paper, and trace the outline of almost anything on it, without relation to the contours of the stone itself.

Painting bottles and glasses

The bottles, jars and glasses you see here cost next to nothing to paint. Once they were just a nuisance collecting dust. Now they are useful and attractive. Small coffee jars make good spice containers. Yoghurt cups are just right for paper clips and rubber bands. A sprig of blossom looks splendid in a wine bottle.

Collect all the jars and bottles you can: orange juice and baby food, vegetable and jam jars; unusually shaped wine and liqueur bottles.

For next to nothing your local glazier will cut off an ugly bottle neck and polish the surface of the jar for you. (Some handicrafts shops will sell you the tools to do it yourself). Then, once they're rinsed and dried, the bottles and jars are ready for a coat of paint.

Your friends will soon prefer your glass gifts to short-lived flowers. Turn your and their junk to good account. The instructions show how easy it is. The pictures will give

These striking designs are examples of modern op-art.

you plenty of ideas which you can copy or use as inspirations for your own original designs.

Brushes – Cleaning fluid

Brushes and paint are all you need to start with. But not all paints are suitable for glass work. When you buy them, ask if they will take on jars and bottles.

In addition to good, standard lacquers you can use poster paints. Paint them over with an appropriate lacquer or varnish once they are dry. You can also use household or decorator's paints, but they dry slowly. To

make sure that the paint or lacquer adheres properly, clean the bottles carefully with alcohol/white spirit or baking/washing soda.

Ordinary hair or bristle watercolor brushes are fine for this kind of painting. If you want to decorate a bottle or glass with small flowers or tiny patterns, use sable brushes. They are expensive but excellent for intricate work.

It is best to have a choice of three different types of brush. For some patterns you will need a $\frac{1}{4}''$–$\frac{1}{2}''$ (6–12 mm) wide bristle brush. The quality of the brushes you choose depends, of course, on your pocket and how often you intend to use them. Always clean your brushes with turpentine, turpentine substitute, or a similar substance immediately after use.

The undercoat

Apply the undercoat, preferably in one color, when the bottles have been perfectly washed and dried. An undercoat is necessary even when the final pattern covers the entire surface. Most paints dry very quickly, so finish the undercoat reasonably fast and in one sitting. Slow or sub-standard work at this stage may result in a spotty surface. To undercoat only part of the bottle, use masking-tape to mark the borders. You must still allow one or two days for the undercoat to dry before painting the final pattern. This ensures that the colors do not run into one another.

Similar care is needed when painting different colors next to one another. A new color

Adapt your flower designs to the shape of the bottle. A flowing pattern is right for a long, slender bottle. In the case of a more angular bottle use the corners to emphasize a petal pattern.

Exciting patterns result from allowing drops of paint to run on the glass. Do this with colors that merge into one another – through the color range from dark red to orange and yellow, for example. By continually adding white, the color scale can be extended to a range of harmonious tones.

can be added only when the one next to it is absolutely dry.

You can make a simple but effective splash of color by giving the bottle only one coat.

Thick glass bottles and jars can be given an inside as well as an outside coat of paint by pouring in the paint and turning the bottle or jar until the whole of the inner surface is covered. As you can see from page 11, the result of this technique is that the outside pattern casts interesting shadows through the thick glass onto the painted inner surface.

Brighten up your parties with gaily-colored wine glasses. Many bottles make excellent vases once the neck has been cut off. This is a job a layman can do himself, although for the subsequent polishing he will have to turn to a glazier.

Elegant pots and bottles can be picked up for a song. The covered pot shown in this picture (top row, second left) was bought at a sale. By careful choice of pattern the unusual bulbous neck of the bottle at bottom left has been used to the full. Paint geometric patterns with the greatest care. Draw the outlines first with a soft pencil.

Patterns for pleasure

Whatever the purpose of the containers (to hold pencils, cigarettes, nuts or cards; to be used as a spice jar, a vase, or a candlestick), the decorative pattern must always suit the room décor.

Stylized flower patterns made up of dots have a pleasing effect and are easy to paint. The bold colors or muted tones of the patterns found on summer dresses can be used with good effect.

Geometric patterns (see middle right) have to be painted with great care. First draw the outlines on the undercoat with a soft pencil. Groups of lines, rectangles (bottom row center) and large and small squares and circles are arresting, and if imaginatively done look interesting. But if birds or fish are chosen as decorations, it is best to cut a stencil and then carefully transfer it. You may prefer to begin with stripes.

To draw faces first make sketches on paper. Then, using a soft pencil, transfer the sketches to the undercoat. With more experience you can paint straight onto the bottle. If you avoid overlapping different shades, you can produce a splendid container in half an hour. Otherwise allow adequate time for drying.

Op-art

This is a fairly new and quite simple variation on usual forms of bottle decoration. In the illustrations on page 12, the patterns themselves appear to set flat surfaces in motion.

19

Faces drawn on jars and bottles can be a great spur to tidiness. They will encourage children to keep their pencils and paintbrushes in good order. In the bathroom, faces look very appealing on containers for skin lotions, hair curlers, bath salts, and so on. For that reason, rather than a riot of color, choose combinations of black and white, or

gray and white, or patterns made up of all three colors.

Though they are decorative in themselves, if you want to use op-art bottles and glasses as vases, then a single flower is most effective in them. Avoid placing op-art objects where they could clash with elaborately patterned floral or similarly inappropriate backgrounds.

Painting on glass

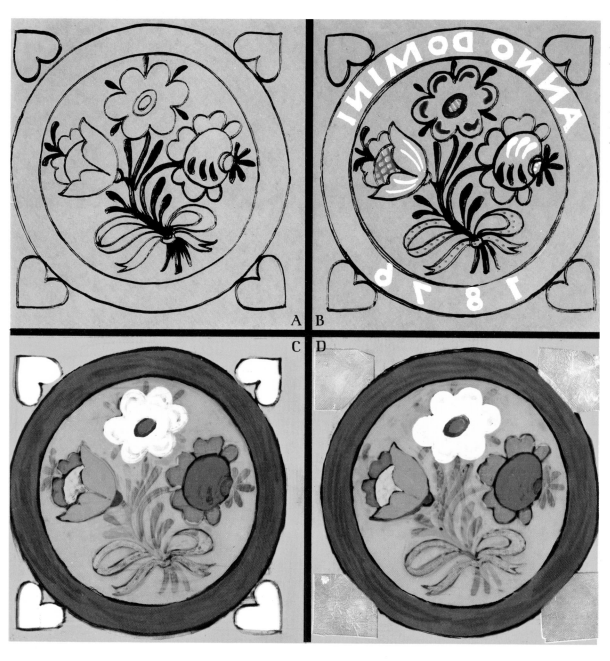

A B
C D

Script must be painted onto the glass in reverse order, back to front. Lay tracing paper on the required letters or figures and draw the outlines with a sharp pencil. Then reverse the tracing paper and place it beneath the glass so that the text can be copied in reverse order with a paint-brush. You can design your own letters or select a script of your choice.

Painting pictures on glass is an entertaining and artistic handicraft. It takes little time and few materials. You don't need much drawing skill. Children love glass painting; it's popular with older people; and pictures on glass make excellent gifts.

The special attraction of a picture painted on the back of a sheet of glass lies in its simple lines and bright colors. The end product is unusually appealing, looks valuable, and has a unique charm.

Adults and children can produce a picture on glass in a very short time, especially if they follow the designs shown here, which are largely based on folk art.

Around the year 1800, painting on glass reached its peak and today these mid-European products are highly popular with art-collectors. Many museums and churches contain examples of baroque art of this kind.

Interest in painting on glass has remained alive in many countries until the present day.

Using their own ideas and designs, young people can create entirely personal decorations based on traditional models.

Use a soft pencil to sketch (on paper) the picture you have in mind. Draw it simply, with firm, clear lines. Ask a glazier to cut a piece of window glass ($\frac{1}{10}''$ or 2–3 mm thick) to the required size. The glass should overlap the sketch by about $\frac{1}{2}''$ (1 cm) at the sides.

With a soft cloth dipped in solvent, rub the glass clean of dust and fingerprints. Then lay it over the sketch with the clean surface upwards. The drawing should be small enough to allow space for a frame round the edge of the glass sheet.

Now, using watercolors or water-resistant ink, copy or trace the outlines of the sketch onto the glass with a fine paintbrush (No. 1 or 2). Clean the brush thoroughly afterwards.

As soon as the paint is dry, fill in lights and shadows with the brush, using poster paint or any paint your art materials or crafts shop recommends. Allow to dry thoroughly.

Sections of the painting which you want to

appear in the foreground must be completed first: that is, paint from front to back. Ornamental initial letters or other script should also be painted at this stage. Paint them in reverse, so that they look right when the glass is turned round.

Now fill the areas framed by black lines with colors of your choice (paint over the lights and shadows). All kinds of opaque watercolors are suitable, but don't spread them too thinly. If you have only red, blue and yellow (apart from black and white) you can produce any shade you like by mixing.

Start adding gold and silver, using silver paper (from chocolate bars, cigarette packets, and so on), aluminium foil, or colored paper. Dab spots of glue in two corners of the area intended for the painting and lay the foil on top.

The charm of old paintings on glass is largely due to the uneven, often greenish glass which the artists employed. Weathering

In old pictures the faces of saints are kept as simple as possible, while their garments are decorative. For the clothes, apply paints flat without shading.

24

has often caused fine cracks to appear in the paint. In many cases genuine gold leaf was used for decoration, although gold paint was sometimes used as a substitute.

By recreating those effects you can produce an old-style painting on glass. But don't forget that the old artists had secrets and techniques which are not fully understood even today, or have been forgotten altogether, so your products will not surpass the originals.

You can sometimes buy "antique glass" from the glazier. But it is expensive, and you may prefer to buy old glass from an antique shop. The glass should be primed with drawing varnish according to instructions on the container (ask at your art materials shop). Once the varnish is dry it will reveal cracks which can be seen through the paint. When the picture is finished this will give the impression that the paint has cracked.

In old German and Austrian glass paintings (which have mainly religious themes) gold

Trace a flower of your choice, enlarge it, add leaves and a stem and paint it onto the glass. Behind the flower you can use silver foil instead of paint. Then the picture looks as if it is painted on a mirror.

leaf was used for haloes, bishops' mitres, crowns and helmets.

Since gold leaf is difficult to apply, imitate the old artists by using gold (or bronze) paint. Remember to keep faces as simple as possible.

Why not paint the saint or individual after whom you are named? Almost every saint has some special symbol (or attribute) related to his or her life. Ask your local library for a book on the subject. There is almost always some familiar item of dress or an instantly recognizable object connected with other famous people which you can reproduce in simple outline.

For the wooden frame go to a carpenter, or a lumber/timber yard. You will need the precise size of the glass and the cross-section of the frame. A strip of felt ($\frac{3}{10}$″ or 7.5 mm wide) must be attached around the inside edge of the frame so that the glass and protective cardboard can be laid in. Stain or paint the frame in the preferred color. The old glass paintings had brown and black frames.

Fix a picture hanger in the middle of the top frame edge with two nails or small screws. Now position the painting carefully inside the frame with the unpainted side of the glass in front. Lay the card on top. Four thin wire tacks, to hold in painting and cardboard, may then be fastened into the felt at each side.

It is just as attractive (and much cheaper) to make your own frame from adhesive tape, or *passe partout*. You can buy this in many colors and widths. Cover the painting with an even piece of cardboard ($\frac{1}{10}$″ or 3 mm thick) and put a hanger at the top.

This copy of an old painting represents Saint Wendelin of Sandl, and comes from 19th-century Austria.

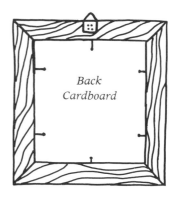

Back Cardboard

Groove
Glass
Cardboard
Pin or nail
Section through wooden frame

Painting china

Painting a set of tea-cups or a dinner service in your favorite colors with designs to match your furniture or your curtains is an unusual but entirely practicable notion.

It is not as difficult as you may think, for white china is available in almost all ceramics or china shops. When ''fired'' at 800° C (1472° F) the paint and glaze merge to form a durable pattern. Today, with so many do-it-yourself kilns on sale and with large kilns in most schools, almost anyone can turn out painted china.

Some shops in large towns and in cities include kilns for hire in their stock. Occasionally institutions allow you to take or send your painted china to them for firing in their kilns. Do-it-yourself kilns designed for enamel-ware pottery are also suitable for this handicraft.

But don't forget that pottery and painted china must never be fired together or the paintwork will be adversely affected by fumes. Each requires a different temperature.

Dust is the arch-enemy of china painting,

so bear that in mind when choosing a work-place. Pick a north-facing window if possible, so that light falls from behind you or from the left. A plastic table cloth will protect a polished table if you spill the turpentine, and it's a good idea to wear a smock or apron for the sake of your clothes. You may also find that you work better when supporting your brush-arm on a book or some other rest.

Start with plain ordinary white china which you can obtain anywhere. At this stage it does not have to be an expensive or high-quality type. But keep clear of used china, since the factory glaze tends to chip imperceptibly and this can lead to ugly marks after the firing process. You need special paints for ''ivory'' china.

Painting materials may be bought as beginner's sets from art materials shops. But you may prefer to assemble your own collection from the rich variety of paints now available.

Paints for china come in tubes, jars and in powder form. The powder paints are best.

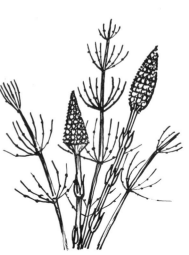

Tube paints easily resinify or become gummy, and are then useless, whereas the jars are expensive to use and are not so effective. Keep your powder paints in dry screw-top jars or in the plastic drums used for pills and films.

It is important to mark the paint containers at once, since you cannot always guess the color after firing merely by looking at the powder. Many dull colors gleam and sparkle only after firing. Because of this change you should fire samples of paint smeared on a plate. Paint your colors through the range from yellow to black at the edge of the plate, and mark each paint for reference. It's a good idea to apply every color both thin and thick to establish a possible variation in shades. If paint is applied too thickly it will burst in the kiln and damage the glaze.

Powder paints are prepared with oil. You can use fat oil, lavender oil or silk-screen printing oil, which is very good to work with. These must be kept absolutely free of dust.

You ought to add drops of pure turpentine

You can paint on faience as well as normal hard china. Tiles, for example, are very suitable for beginners because of their even surface. But you will soon get used to the uneven curved surfaces of bowls and plates. When buying china choose smooth simple forms suitable for decoration. Ribbed china or china bearing a relief is unsuitable for beginners. Before painting rinse the china in warm water, otherwise it needs no preparation.

when you are actually painting. It is also essential for cleaning brushes. But be sure to use the real thing; avoid turpentine substitutes.

The turpentine should be poured into a china egg cup, since the smooth curving sides are ideal for wiping and washing brushes. Don't be stingy with the turpentine, since paints are all the better for being applied with a brush which has been thoroughly cleaned. After painting, cover the turpentine container with aluminium foil or a lid. Use turpentine to remove any paint you spill on the floor.

There is a wide selection of brushes to choose from, but at first you can manage with only a few. Short quill brushes are best suited for painting china. Lengthen the brush by attaching it to a wooden skewer. Use the pointed end as a "compass" when painting.

The better you treat your brushes the longer you will enjoy using them. Only when they are "broken in" do paintbrushes give of their best. Every time you change the paint clean your brush properly with lots of turpentine, or impure colors will result. If any paint left on the brush dries and hardens, soften it up slowly in turpentine. Keep the brush in a jar with the pointed end up.

Finally, you will need a spatula with a flexible tip for mixing paints and a plate of glass (4″ × 8″, 10 × 20 cm) with one rough surface. A color or pigment grinder is not absolutely essential but well worth having. China paint pots from art materials shops also come in useful since they can be stored one above the other.

Use the spatula to place just enough paint powder for one or two days' painting on the rough side of the glass plate. Add a few drops of silkscreen-printing oil, and mix the paint with the spatula held flat and knead it until no more paint grains are visible. Mixing is even better with a paint-grinder. Keep collecting the paint into a small heap with the spatula until it is thick and as viscous as dough. Then push the paint into a corner of the glass, leaving plenty of free space in which to add turpentine.

Turpentine evaporates, so keep adding a little from time to time. Paint that is properly mixed should spread easily and can be shaded off, but it must not be runny. Since each paint is different it is not possible to give precise proportions of paint to oil. But it is better to paint too dry than too oily.

Closely-related colors mix well with each other. Green, for example, turns brighter and warmer with yellow, but dull and cold with blue. Red goes only with brown. Many colors – such as yellow – completely absorb colors added during the kiln process. To obtain orange, for example, you must paint with yellow and add a coat of red after the first firing.

Soak your brush in turpentine, dry it on a smooth cloth (e.g., linen), and with the tip of the brush (never fill the brush with paint up to the handle) take paint from the edge of the heap and soften it up with a drop of turpentine. Now paint away at your leisure. The great advantage of painting china is that you can wipe it all off as often as you like. Any imprecise lines or too heavily painted areas can be corrected with a brush that has been rinsed and dried.

Start afresh as often as you wish before the object is fired. Don't get impatient if the brush doesn't do as it's told immediately. Dry paint can be made pliable again with a drop of turpentine.

You can draw designs on the china by using a china-marker or similar pencil. The pencil mark will disappear without trace in the firing. Ball points, soft-tip or felt pens and copying pencils should not be used since they leave permanent marks.

To make a tracing (transferring a design from paper on to the china), draw the design you require on thin transparent paper: greaseproof paper will do. Then, with graphite powder or with a soft pencil held flat, rub the reverse of the tracing and stick it on to the china with adhesive tape. Using a hard pencil you can easily transfer the drawing to the china.

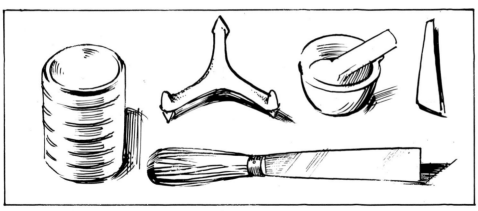

It is best to let freshly painted china dry out at a low temperature in the kitchen oven for about half an hour. The paint is then resistant to dust. It doesn't matter if the colors have slightly changed.

To be of practical use the painted objects must be fired at a temperature of 780°–820° C (1436°–1508° F). The glaze softens and the paint sinks into it.

To make best possible use of your kiln space, you can try kiln accessories such as bats, and stilts made from fire-resistant clay on which to place the china. The stilts must not rest on any paintwork or they will stick fast in the kiln during the firing process. Faience and tiles should not come into contact with stilts or the glaze may be damaged.

If your kiln has no pyrometer for measuring the temperature, you will have to use a cone placed in the kiln behind the window. These cones are made in such a way that they fall over at a given temperature and the kiln must

If you want to repeat a design several times, draw the design on transparent paper and, working on a pile of newspapers, prick out the lines with a needle. Smooth down the back of the tracing with fine sandpaper to remove the uneven prick marks, then stick the tracing on the china with adhesive tape.
Take a small wad of cotton wool or absorbent cotton, dust it with graphite powder (which can be obtained by rubbing a soft pencil on sandpaper) and wipe it over the tracing. Remove the tracing carefully and underneath you will find a dot-for-dot outline on the china.

then be switched off. China is placed in a cold kiln and is taken out once the kiln has cooled down again.

Embed the cone in a stiff paste of powdered fire-clay and water on a small prop or fragment of pot so that you can see it through the window. To let oil fumes escape, leave the damper, the window or the door ajar until the interior begins to glow (at about 400°–500° C; 750°–950° F), then close everything and wait for the desired temperature, i.e. the fall of the cone. With small do-it-yourself kilns use cone 015a; in the larger kilns you can also use 014a.

It doesn't really matter what you paint at first. The important thing is to become acquainted with the painting technique. Start off with one or two colors. Meissen red, for example, is color-fast, good to work with and simpler to shade off than blue. If you use black as a second color there are some attractive contrasts.

After the first firing of your painted china you will be very pleased at the way the paints gleam once they have combined with the glaze. But on closer examination, especially when you're just starting, you may notice that the paints are too light and the lines blurred. You can obtain darker shades by adding another coat of paint, and a drawing pen may be used to emphasize certain details. Then, with a second or even third firing, a well-designed piece of china will become clearer and more expressive.

Make a drawing of anything which strikes you as an attractive theme. A painter's sketchbook is like a store-room into which he can always peep. With flowers or animals the best plan is always to draw from nature, perhaps by copying a realistic painting. If you're fond of famous old china make an effort to copy the patterns as accurately as possible. This is just one way of learning how to paint. But don't be discouraged if it doesn't turn out immediately as planned.

If you like ornamental painting, nature is an inexhaustible source of themes. A magnifying glass comes in very useful if you're

on the lookout for designs in the countryside.

With geometric models aim at a good design arrangement on the object to be painted. If you want to draw attention to certain aspects of the design it is essential to paint precisely.

Always bear in mind that your painting should emphasize the form of the china. The round shape of a plate is ruined by vertical or horizontal lines. Similarly you must adapt the pattern on an oblong dish to the shape.

When painting a vase don't forget its purpose. You don't want your painting to clash with the flowers. Good effect depends on a well-balanced pattern adapted to the shape of the china. You can have lines radiating from the center-point or from anywhere else, but the balance must be right.

You can paint anything on china that you would paint on paper or on other materials. But of course the shape and type of china, its purpose and the technique you use all play a part in the choice of design.

34

There is no need to restrict your painting to white surfaces. You may prefer a colored surface. For this we recommend light colored tiles, which can easily be obtained at low prices in crafts supply shops. The best paints to use would be black, brown or a dark color related to the tile's own color. Tiles are pleasant to paint and have many uses. You can frame them as pictures or use them to stand things on. You can make them into trays and table tops.

Easy enamelling

This unusual but highly-decorative handicraft technique involves the use of ordinary nail-lacquer, polish or varnish. You apply the lacquer, together with ink, to copper or brass. The effect is similar to that of enamel, but there is no tiresome firing process.

All you have to do is to dab the lacquer on. No brushwork is necessary. First clean and prepare the copper surface with acetone so that attractive patterns form when you apply the lacquer. After covering the prepared copper blank (obtainable from handicrafts shops) with a layer of clear lacquer, paint it over with colored soft-tipped pens. Alternatively, color the white pearlized lacquer with ink. If you allow the different patches of color

to run into each other while still wet, almost endless variations will result. You can use any kind of pearlized lacquer. The more expensive ones dry especially hard, while the cheaper varieties are easier to work and are more transparent.

If you add acetone you can change the quality of the lacquer. Test this by putting two drops of lacquer and one drop of acetone into a small dish or lid. The lacquer changes immediately. It first expands to form a circle or a star, and then contracts to form con-tinually changing patterns with a delicate veining rather like a leaf or a butterfly's wings.

This process enables you to produce attractive jewelry to match the colors of the clothes you want to wear them with. You can also make boxes of various sizes (the illustrations show only the box lids), small plates and dishes, tins for sweets and candies, and match-box holders, and so on. Only ash-trays are excluded because the lacquer is not heat-resistant.

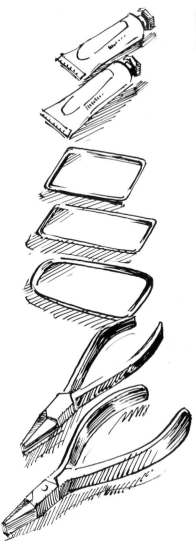

To mix your colors you can either dye the white lacquer with drawing-ink, or color the copper beforehand with soft-tipped pens. Add two to four drops of ink to half a bottle of lacquer. This is best done with a pipette or glass dropper as too much ink spoils the lacquer and makes the color too dark. The bottle should be well shaken – sideways rather than up and down. It may take several hours before the lacquer is uniformly colored. You may also find that it becomes somewhat darker after a couple of days. Since the white content of lacquer tends to make colors somewhat harsher and brighter, it is impossible to produce subtle orange and tangerine tones in this way. But since nail lacquer is available in a wide range of good reds this really does not pose a problem.

Always mix your colors in the bottle, never in a dish, because lacquer dries fast when exposed to air. For the same reason, paint directly from the bottle. Hence you should collect as many empty bottles and small metal containers with lids as you can. Because the

quantities involved are so small, you can mix your inks in small dishes or lids. The primary colors – red, yellow and blue – will be adequate for most purposes. Once mixed, add these combined colors immediately, drop by drop, to the lacquer in the bottle. Combine different colored lacquers only on the copper surface itself. (Don't add more ink directly onto the copper, as that causes small craters in the lacquer.)

After applying the first color, dab the second one on. If the colors don't mix prop-erly, add another drop of acetone carefully to the layer of lacquer you have already applied. Remember that colors thinned with acetone take longer to dry than plain lacquer. You can use white lacquer on its own, but first color the ground with soft-tipped pens. Prepare the copper in the usual way and apply a layer of clear lacquer. When that is dry, color the surface with soft-tipped pens (without the lacquer undercoat the colors will not adhere to the copper). If you dab the white lacquer on carefully, it will mix with the prepared ground to form a delightful maze of patterns. Soft-tipped pens are especially suitable for this type of grounding.

Interesting effects result when you allow a number of colors to run freely into each other. Choose two or more contrasting colors, or simply various tones of the same color. First paint the whole surface with one of the colors. While it is still wet, dab on the second color. The colors will mix immediately to produce small patterns and color patches that create more effects where they overlap at the edges. Only colored lacquers are suitable for this process. Grounding with soft-tipped pens does not produce such dramatic effects.

In the controlled blending technique you dab the colors on side by side. You will find an example of this in the scent bottle shown here. You put a diagonal band of two shades of blue-green between two areas of white lacquer, all blending softly into each other to create interesting patterns and half-tones. In brush-blending, apply a large number of colored dots and strokes side by side. Then add one or two drops of acetone from a pipette and mix all the colors together with a fine camel-hair brush. But don't use the brush from the lacquer bottle. This technique was used to make the pendant shown here. Another particularly attractive example is the small dish, for which the colours were dabbed onto a ground already prepared with lacquer. A couple of drops of acetone were added and the design was then applied with a brush.

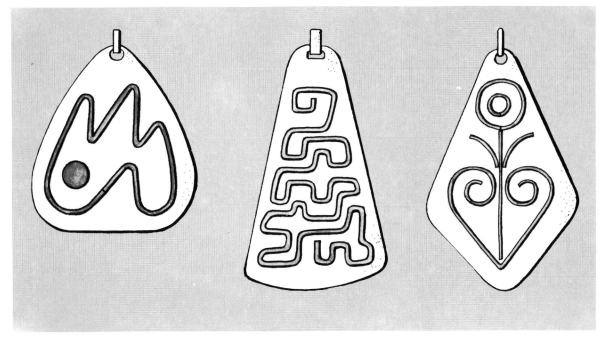

Copper blanks are obtainable in all handicraft shops. You can get pieces of copper sheet and match-box containers cut to your specification at most hardware stores, though it is advisable to supply a detailed sketch and the precise measurements you want.

Such motifs as birds or fishes are easy to execute if you make a small sketch beforehand on a piece of paper. Ready-made wire loops generally have an opening but can be made into full circles by bending them with round-nosed pliers. You can introduce further variety by using the larger loops available from haberdashers and handicrafts dealers.

Once you have made an attractive design from the wire, fix it with clear lacquer to the copper blank. To do this first dip a fine camel-hair brush into the lacquer and allow it to dry (i.e. harden). Then dip this hardened brush-point gently into the lacquer. Hold the brush upright above the work and without touching the ring, and allow a small drop to fall into the loop. The wire pieces and loops must lie absolutely flat on the copper, otherwise the liquid will spill over the edges. If there is too much lacquer in a loop you can soak up the excess with a small roll of newspaper.

Two hours later glue the rings on firmly. You can now work over the ground and fill

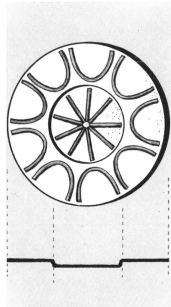

the rings with drops of coloured lacquer. If, after drying, you find the lacquer is still below the level of the loop, add a couple more drops of the same color.

When the upper surface of the work has dried you can lacquer the edges, but be sure to use the side rather than the tip of the brush. Remember to shake the bottle of lacquer vigorously with a sideways motion before use. Always keep the neck of the bottle clean, otherwise you will have difficulty opening it. The simplest way of avoiding this problem is to clean the neck of each bottle with acetone every time you have finished using it. For cloisonné work, buy 0.4 mm (0.016″ = 20 gauge) copper wire, as it can be easily bent with the fingers. Place the object to be decorated on a piece of paper, trace round it with a pencil and then sketch in your design within the shape of the outline. Next shape the wire to match the lines of your design, taking care to press it flat in the curves. Place the finished wire pattern between two boards and hammer firmly on the top board until the wire pattern

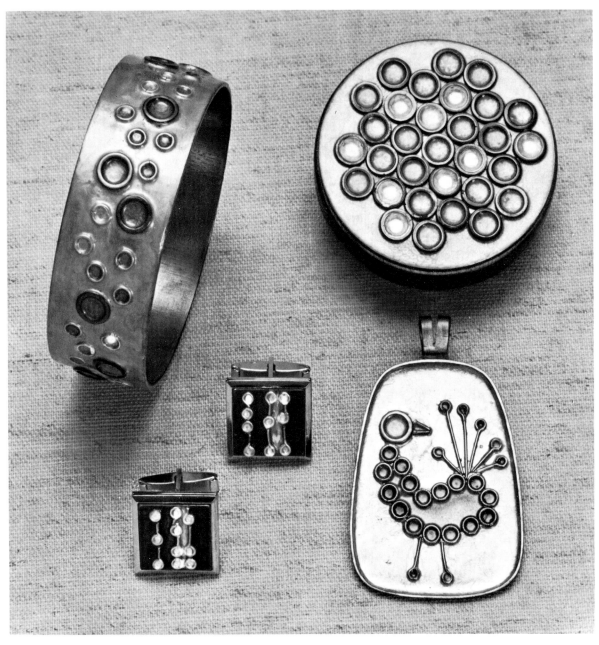

You can clean off any unsatisfactory items with a rag dipped in acetone, though a few isolated spots may not come off, especially where repeated layers of lacquer have hardened to form a solid mass like drops of candle-wax. Remove any grease remaining on the copper with alcohol. When dry, paint the whole surface with acetone, being very careful not to touch it with bare fingers.

Ringlet work is not difficult. The silver wire rods and rings you need are also obtainable in handicraft shops. Place a prepared copper blank on the table and arrange the fine pieces of silver wire on it to make whatever pattern you wish. You can use any motif from a decorative star to an abstract design. Alternatively, you can scatter the rings over the whole surface. Hooks can be bent by hand, though you will find that a pair of smooth pliers comes in useful. Or you can always bend them open with a pair of old scissors to form any number of different patterns and shapes.

Having finished the patterned surface, complete the work by cleaning the other side with a brass or silver cleaner. But don't let the cleaning agent come into contact with the lacquer on the front. Finally, give the entire surface a coating of transparent varnish. Attach brooch clasps with glue, following the manufacturer's directions.

is flat enough to glue to the copper blank. You can only buy 0.5 mm (0.019″) gauge silver wire and it can be bent into the desired forms only with round-nosed pliers. Follow the directions on the tube and apply a thin layer of glue (e.g. Araldite in the UK; gum tragacanth in US) to the prepared copper blank. Place the wire ornament onto this and press it in firmly. You should leave the work under a weight for 24 hours so that the wire is firmly glued in place throughout. You are then ready to apply a layer of paint – a single color or several colors, as you wish – to both the ground and the areas marked by wire.

For painting with lacquer you need copper blanks, white lacquer, red, blue and yellow drawing inks, gold-bronze, two very fine brushes, a bottle of acetone, silver wire rods and loops, clear nail-lacquer, and glue, used strictly in accordance with the manufacturer's directions. For cloisonné work you also need copper or silver wire (0.4 or 0.5 mm gauge; 0.016″ or 0.019″), soft-tipped pens, a pipette, smooth pliers, and nail-lacquers.

42

Painting wood

A wide range of plain, unpainted wooden articles is offered in hardware, hobby and handicraft shops, and you can transform all of these with a coat of paint in a cheerful color. The safest thing is to paint each article in a single color as this way there is no risk of bad clashes. A plain wooden candlestick, for example, painted a deep orange, brings a brilliant splash of color to the room. But for those who want to add a more personal touch, this chapter will give you plenty of ideas as well as explaining the different techniques you can use.

Articles made of wood which haven't already been painted, oiled or stained are easiest to work. Choose a good covering paint (poster paints are ideal). But there are many hard-wearing paints – consult your dealer. All these paints are easy to use, can be thinned with water and painted over with other colors. They dry quickly and evenly in 20 minutes with a light velvety finish. Once dry they are waterproof and can be painted over. They are easier to use than oil or gloss paints and there is less danger of obliterating different parts of the pattern as you add a new color.

Before starting, stir the paint, and thin it if necessary with a little water. After use, keep the paint containers tightly shut. A drop of water in each will help to keep them airtight and prevent the paint drying up and becoming too thick. If that happens, remove any dried-up paint immediately from the lid and sides of the containers with a brush and a little water.

You should prime the wood with a coat of white paint to prevent darkening and absorption of the color later. It is easier to apply subsequent colors to an undercoat; this maintains the brightness and subtle gradations of color that enhance the appearance of, say, flower patterns. To avoid spoiling the work area spread out a few sheets of newspaper before starting.

First sandpaper the wood using fine sandpaper, and brush away all the dust. Apply the white paint evenly (thinned if necessary) and leave to dry, preferably overnight, in a warm room. If you are going to paint more than one article, apply the white undercoat to all of them at this stage. You can then leave them until you have the time and leisure to concentrate on the final design.

To ensure the highest quality finish, it is worth adding a second undercoat. First sandpaper the original coat with very fine sandpaper, removing all the dust with a brush or soft cloth. Apply the second coat and leave overnight so it is thoroughly dry. You can of course dispense with the second coat of white paint if you have chosen an undercoat suitable for a topcoat. But if you do apply two undercoats you will find the extra effort amply rewarded in the enhanced appearance and durability of the finished work.

The next stage is to select the colors. Decide on a plain color for the background and a color combination for the central motif.

Candlestick
The old-fashioned shape was made by turning on a lathe. It was decorated in oil paint in green ochre, blue-green and pink.

Spoon
Base in blue poster paint with dot and flower motif added in matching colors and finally finished with a coat of clear lacquer.

Here you should bear in mind both the article's use and its prospective place in the home. It should either blend in harmony with the surroundings or effect a strong contrast. In a light room with a lot of white, strong fluorescent colors are best: orange, turquoise, rose pink and leaf green. Think of the person you're going to give the article to. Perhaps you know his or her favorite color.

An imaginative person will quickly come up with some original and attractive designs. But everyone can draw inspiration from the wide range of pretty printed materials, wallpapers and wrapping paper to be found today. Once you have begun to work at this handicraft, you will quickly acquire an eye for the beauty all around you whether it is in the forms and colors of nature or in paintings and other works of art.

If the wood has a fine grain, it is a pity not to let it show, so simply use a transparent glaze for the undercoat. You can paint the central motif with an ordinary emulsion, but dilute it first with water (one part water to

45

one part paint). Too thin paint is not so hard-wearing. You can also use colored wood stain or any of the special transparent paints available. The chipwood box illustrated here has been given an application of colored glaze and finished off with a lacquer. Alternatively you can use a colored glaze or transparent paint for the motif, giving a very effective contrast with the plain background. The chipwood box has an orange background and the initials are painted in pastel.

You can also make a bold striped design by

Napkin rings are a welcome gift, especially a set with a distinctive pattern for each member of the family and for guests.

using masking tape. Paint the article in a color of your choice and leave it overnight to dry. Lay the narrow strips of masking tape (e.g., 1–2 cm, $\frac{1}{2}''$–$\frac{3}{4}''$, wide) across or round the article. Work from the center outwards, and press them down firmly. Now repaint the article in a second color and once more leave it to dry overnight. The next day, carefully remove the masking tape to reveal the attractive stripes in the original color. Touch up any unevenness of line, and decorate one set of stripes with dots in a matching or contrasting color. You can also attach masking tape to any metal fittings that cannot be easily removed (the hook on a clothes hanger for example). This is a precaution worth taking as you don't have the subsequent difficulty of trying to remove the paint from the metal.

Many people feel more at home with scissors and paper than with paint and brush. A good technique is to draw the round or oval shape of a chipwood box somewhat smaller on a piece of paper. Fold the paper down the center once or twice and cut some imaginative shapes into it. Unfolding and

smoothing out the paper will reveal more interesting patterns and designs than many a person could achieve by drawing. The cut-out shapes can be used later to decorate something else. Paint a chipwood box, for example, in an attractive color (red, blue or green) and spread the lid and reverse side of the paper cut-out with rubber solution. When this becomes tacky, place the cut-out exactly in the center of the lid and press it firm. You can rub off any excess rubber solution with your finger. Give the lid a protective coat of clear lacquer afterwards.

Begin with simple geometrical shapes – a circle or rectangle; a rhombus or just stripes. Try the design first by sketching it on paper and completing it with your choice of colors. When you are satisfied, draw the lines of the design in pencil on the wooden article you want to decorate and then paint it with the colors you have prepared. If the pattern is an intricate one, it is best to draw it on tracing paper. If the object to be decorated is light in color, then use a pencil to

Wooden box: simple stylized flower design outlined in poster-black. Dark green border (mixed out of blue-green and green) with blue-green markings.

Small tin: olive green (mixed out of ochre, green and yellow). Pure orange lid, upper half pink mixed with white.

Large tin: orange lightened with yellow and reddish violet. Star and borders outlined in black.

Candlestick: blue and orange.

draw along the lines on the reverse side of the paper. If however, the base color is dark, then do it in chalk or a light-colored crayon, before transferring the design from the tracing paper with a hard pencil or empty ballpoint pen. For greater accuracy, fix the edge of the tracing paper with masking tape to the surface of the object.

If you are going to mix your own colors, it is best to do it in a screw-top jar. Transfer the paint with a wooden spatula and mix it well using a broad-bristle brush. Always mix enough paint; if you run out it will be difficult to match the identical color. Mix more paint than you think you need, so that you have some over for making corrections. In order to ensure an even application, the paint should be neither too thick nor too watery. The basic rule is that the first coat should be applied thinly and left to dry for 2–4 hours. The second application can be of a thicker consistency.

Painting wooden boxes

What we said in the last chapter about paints and working methods applies to painting boxes. In this chapter we concentrate on modern designs and finishing techniques.

The pictures shown in this section will give you some ideas for various ways of painting boxes. They come from professional artists, amateurs and children.

The examples are not restricted to folk themes, although folk art is a goldmine for motifs: pure geometric borders, stylized

flowers, animals and primitive figure draw-ings. If you live near a museum of decorative arts or an ethnological museum, you will find plenty of ideas there. But your own fantasy is a good source of designs too.

After making a few rough sketches, lay the box on transparent paper and draw round it with pencil; then, after removing the box, sketch your theme on the paper.

Attach the drawing to the box with ad-hesive tape. Use graphite paper (but not carbon paper) to trace the drawing onto the lid.

If you haven't any graphite paper, you can trace the outline on to the reverse side of the drawing paper with a soft pencil – or white chalk on a dark background – and then impress the drawing onto the box with a tracing needle. You can also use a dead ball-point pen or a hard pencil. With practice you should be able to draw on the box with a soft pencil and then paint freely.

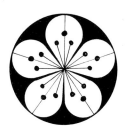

Geometric themes

Draw the design directly on the box, then follow round the sketch with a ruler and compass.

A circular shape is a good design basis for a round or oval-shaped box. Circles are also a good starting point for many themes: spirals, rosettes, flowers and stars.

Playing with geometric forms

Op-Art and computer drawing show the influence of our technical age on the fine arts.

Op-Art in particular has emphasized the harmony of geometrical and symmetrical shapes. Typical characteristics of Op-Art are: abstract, purely geometric shapes, mechanical structures, controlled shimmering effects through the use of strong color contrasts (e.g., contrasting red and green, or black and white), highly symmetrical arrangements and precise execution.

Anyone accustomed to using ruler, compasses and set square will be fascinated by

51

Gold patina work

Working method

Put the gold leaf on a soft surface (e.g., a newspaper), trace on the theme, and impress the drawing in front and behind with a tracing needle or a dead ballpoint pen; then apply the patina, cut out the drawing and stick it on the box. Double-sided adhesive film is good for sticking on the paper. Remove the top covering leaf of the adhesive film, stick on the motif and cut it out exactly. Then remove the lower covering leaf and stick the motif onto the painted background of the box. Use a tracing needle to impress parts of the ornamentation again, particularly if the patina is too dark in the grooves. In this way the finest indentation will stick fast without leaving behind unpleasant traces of adhesive. Cut out the top motif by folding the paper.

Jewelry box

The woman's head was first painted onto a violet background. If you can't paint this, take a portrait photograph, and surround it with a foil frame. Cut this by folding the sheet until you get a symmetrical shape.

Side of box

Decorated above with a strip of gold foil; painted below in violet; gold patina.

the harmony of geometrical shapes and their internal laws. Little imagination or mathematical knowledge is needed to discover new designs and variations.

Designs are also offered by the various "pin-and-thread" or string-craft products which are so popular at present. The linear designs are filled alternately with black or white when the box is decorated.

Make a few experimental drawings on paper. Once you have developed a suitable theme, transfer it to a white-primed box.

Circular motifs are best carried out with a pair of compasses containing a drawing pen and black ink or paint. For strict geometrical lines in a black-and-white design it is best to use an India or China ink designer's pen in precision work.

Tips for after-treatment

If you want a matt finish to stay that way it requires no after-treatment. Otherwise "polish" the paint with a soft cloth or a

brush, so that it takes on a dull gleam.

By rubbing in colorless white polishing-wax and buffing the box smooth, the shine will be heightened, the color deepened and the paint protected from drops of water.

You can obtain a glossier polish by using a colorless silk-finish or matt varnish. These varnishes sometimes come in spray cans. Varnishing makes the colors more brilliant.

If you want an "old varnished oil-painting," or "crackle varnish" effect, you can buy ready-to-use kits complete with in-structions. Through repeated application of two special varnishes small cracks will appear on the painted surface, like those on old paintings. These cracks can then be glossed with oil paint, if you have the time and you prize an "antique look."

With a little careful varnishing, boxes bearing rural peasant designs take on that special charm which emanates from old things. Other themes – those with a white background for example – also gain from varnishing. The patina unifies ornamental

53

details and helps to hide minor defects.

If you cannot buy a ready-to-use patina fluid, you can usually have one made up at a paint supplier's (one part linseed oil, one part genuine oil of turpentine, and a little siccative). You will also need a small tube of oil paint: amber, burnt sienna or Vandyke brown; a green-tinted brown shade will give a "green earth" effect.

Take some patina fluid and a little oil paint up on a wad of cloth. Rub the well-dried paintwork evenly with the wad. Rub down

again with a clean cloth after 10 to 20 minutes.

You can keep the background darker and the painted design lighter. If the patina turns out too dark you can lighten it with patina fluid.

You can also give a patina finish to the rough wood of the box if it has a very pleasing grain. The patina must dry out overnight. Then paint on the motifs and give a final patina.

It is advisable to paint the inside of the box with poster paint. It looks attractive and makes the box look more solid. The shade can match the outside background color or can contrast with it.

If the box is to be filled with biscuits (cookies), or sweets (candies), line it with metal foil. The foil can be stuck on. It keeps the contents airtight and fresh. But don't stick anything on the inside lid.

Line small boxes and containers for jewelery, cuff-links, and so on with felt or velvet, and velvet ribbon remnants. You can stick them on with all-purpose glue.

Making games

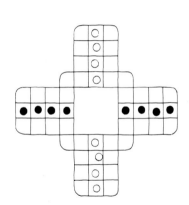

You need: *Two or preferably four players, each with four counters of the same color (it should be easy to put them on top of each other) and a six-sided dice on which the six equals zero.*

The board: *First draw a rectangle at the center of the board, consisting of 25 small squares each 2×2 cm ($\frac{3}{4}'' \times \frac{3}{4}''$). The four squares at the edge should be rounded off and the nine inner*

squares rubbed out. Then adapt the face of the board to form a cross shape in which every arm is a rectangle consisting of nine small squares. In painting these squares the color shades turn lighter as they approach the outside edge.

The great majority of board games exist to provide entertainment and train the mind. The royal tombs at Ur of the Chaldees show that such games were played there about 5000 years ago. A slightly more recent example was found in an Egyptian temple.

We have selected a few prominent examples from a large number of more or less well-known board games which have come down from antiquity. In this chapter we show you how to make them yourself. These are colorful games which you can produce without much trouble. In almost every case the materials are simple and inexpensive.

Roundabout

Rules: Before starting, each player places his

counters on the four light-colored squares of his middle row, working from the middle. Then each player throws in turn, moving his counters in a clockwise direction until they have crossed the starting squares and reached the middle. The aim is to get two, three or four counters together on the same square, since they can then move forward the same number of squares as a single counter. If a player catches up with an opponent's counter – or two or more counters – he chases the opponent back to the starting squares, keeping together any combinations of two or three counters. There are no barriers or enforced rests in this game and the winner is the first player to get all his counters in the middle.

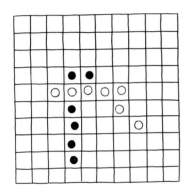

FIVE IN A ROW

You need: *Two players each with either 20 light or dark counters.*

The board: *Draw a rectangle 20 × 20 cm ($7\frac{1}{2}'' × 7\frac{1}{2}''$) and divide it into 100 small squares – each 2 × 2 cm ($\frac{3}{4}'' × \frac{3}{4}''$). The squares should be painted in such a way that they present an overall design. The changing colors are not significant for the rules of the game. They are simply pleasing to the eye, and make it more difficult for the players to obtain a general view of the game.*

Your best home-made games boards can also serve as wall decorations. Just drive a staple carefully into the middle of the board's top edge. It's also worth enquiring at a stationer's about self-adhesive hangers and hooks.

Five in a row

Rules: Start with a clear board. Each player in turn places a counter on the board and tries to form a row of five counters either at right angles to the side or diagonally. A player who succeeds in doing this may take a counter from his opponent – but only if it is standing alone and does not form part of a row of five. When all the counters are on the board they are moved into the adjoining squares in a straight line or diagonally. Each player keeps trying to form new rows of five and to take his opponent's counters. Anyone with only five counters left may hop over his opponent's counters. But a player who is surrounded before hopping, so that he cannot move any counters, has lost the game. So has a player who loses one of his five counters in hopping.

Squares: The size of the board is shown for each game. Allow a few centimeters (approx. 1″) for the border. The dimensions given are not essential. As long as the proportions are the same a board of any size will do.

To make a gameboard, choose 5 or 6 mm ($\frac{1}{4}''$) plywood. Cut it to the right size. Any friendly wood store or timber yard will cut out a board for you at little cost – possibly from wood remnants. If you want to saw plywood it is best to use a fine-toothed saw. Then rub down the wood. Start with medium sandpaper, and follow up with fine. File down the rough edges and rub with sandpaper stretched over a wooden block. The edges will gently crumble away.

Clear all dust from the board. Prime the surface with white paint. Use special water-based primer applied thickly with a broad

brush. If the wood is to remain in its natural state, prime it with cold size thinned down with water.

Watercolors may now be applied to this surface without running. Once the priming paint has dried, you can rub it down once more with fine sandpaper. Prime both sides of the board, even if only one side is to be used for playing. Even plywood tends to warp when damp if only one side has been primed.

If you are good at drawing you can set to work on the board at once. But it is better to draft a plan on paper and transfer it by tracing with carbon paper (not blue carbon) onto the board.

For painting you need opaque paints and watercolors. Opaque paints come in the form of poster paints or other water-based paints, such as gouache. Watercolors can be found in any school paintbox.

The three primary colors will give many shades by careful mixing. With watercolors you can produce intermediate shades by over-painting. Poster paints can be laid over each other. The result is better if each color is

painted separately. With watercolors you must do this in order to avoid mixed colors.

For clear straight lines, use adhesive film or masking tape on the edges of squares you do not intend to paint. Draw lines with a ruler and a fibertip pen. A modern drawing pen will do as well, using China or India ink, or the ink recommended.

Once the board is painted, you can apply a clear varnish. Then matt paints will look brilliant. Varnish protects the surface of the board against scratches and so forth, and the effects of moisture. Apply matt or brilliant varnish freely with a broad painter's brush. Afterwards rinse the brush in paint-thinner or turpentine substitute, otherwise it will turn hard. Varnish also comes in aerosol spray cans. But these are more expensive and harmful to the environment and atmosphere.

Buy brushes of various sizes. Choose the best brushes available – marten-hair brushes if you can. These form very sharp points when they are damp. Use painter's brushes only for priming and varnishing. But make sure that they don't shed their bristles.

The games board can also be made from suitable pieces of chip-board, hard fiber-board or thick pasteboard or cardboard.

Dice

You can use normal six-sided dice for most of the games listed here; but some require a four-sided dice. Make these by getting a square wooden rod (or baluster molding) with a cross-section of about 15 × 15 mm ($\frac{5}{8}'' \times \frac{5}{8}''$), and by sawing off pieces 3 cm ($1\frac{1}{4}''$) in length.

Rub down the square rod with fine sandpaper before sawing. Rub down the sawn surfaces and any slightly broken edges. Then paint on the dice dots. The total of dots on opposite faces must always add up to 5. With normal dice the total of dots on opposite faces should always come to 7.

Counters

Some hobby shops sell machined wooden figures. You can paint these very brightly. But for a completely self-produced board, use

sections cut from a round piece of wood (for instance, a broom handle or a piece of dowel).

Of course you can play with improvised counters (buttons, coins, beans), but only in some games.

Stone's throw

Rules: Light-colored counters are placed on one half of the board and dark counters on the other. The center stays empty.

The aim is to change places. In doing this, each piece may move only one square to an adjoining square or over an opponent's counter if the square beyond is empty. The aim is to get all your counters in the other half of the board in the lowest possible number of moves or hops. If several players compete one after the other, each player's moves may be counted and written down. The player with the lowest number of moves is the overall winner.

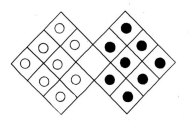

STONE'S THROW

You need: *One player and a few spectators who take their turn later. Eight light and eight dark counters.*

The board: *Draw a rectangle 15 × 15 cm (6¼″ × 6¼″) and divide it into 25 small squares, each 3 × 3 cm (1¼″ × 1¼″). If four squares in both the top right and bottom left corner are rubbed out, 17 squares remain, which you decorate with cats and mice (see illustration). Put a golden star in the center square, which joins both halves of the board.*

59

Fetching honey

Rules: Each player throws in turn. If a blue and a yellow face are shown on the dice the player places a counter on the green hexagon. With one blue and one red face he covers the lilac hexagon; with blue and white the light blue; with red and white, the brown; with blue and blue the dark blue; with yellow and yellow the bright yellow hexagon; and with red and red the bright red one. If a player throws for a square which is already occupied, he can take the piece and throw once more. If he comes to an occupied square again he can take this piece too. He keeps throwing the dice until he reaches an unoccupied hexagon, where he leaves his counter.

With red and red shown on the dice, however, a player may not take the piece on an occupied square but must throw the dice again and collect his pieces later. The fortunate player who throws white and white wins all the pieces on the board. Then he throws once more and places a counter on the appropriate square. If by any chance he throws white and white again, he must occupy all 10 hexagons.

But if another player throws white and white immediately afterwards, he has to sacrifice 10 pieces. Any player who has no counters left must stop playing. The player left at the end takes all the pieces and is the winner.

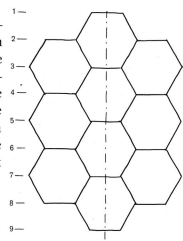

FETCHING HONEY

You need: *As many players as you wish (the more the merrier). Give each player 24 small counters of any type. In addition you need two special dice which should be at least twice as long as a normal dice. These are painted on the four long sides in the colors white, yellow, red and blue. The two square ends may be painted black or remain unpainted.*

The board: *First draw a 20.8 cm (8″) long, vertical guide-line, at the center. At a 90° angle to this line – starting from the top – draw nine shorter, horizontal lines each 2.6 cm in length, or at broad intervals extending about 3″ to each side. Give these lines temporary numbers from 1 to 9. Then mark a dot on the horizontal lines to the right and left of the vertical center-line at the following distance from the center line: on lines 1 and 9 at 1.5 cm ($\frac{9}{16}$″) from the center; on lines 2, 4, 6 and 8 at 3 cm ($1\frac{1}{8}$″) and 6 cm ($2\frac{1}{4}$″); on lines 3, 5, 7 at 1.5 cm ($\frac{9}{16}$″) and 6 cm ($2\frac{9}{16}$″) (once each).*

Now join the dots nearest to each other with lines so that the 10 hexagons shown are formed. When all superfluous guide-lines and numbers have been rubbed out, paint the two center squares

60

red and white, and the eight
outside squares in the series blue,
yellow, light blue, light yellow,
pink, green, orange and lilac.

RAINBOW

*You need: As many players as
you like. Each player receives
between one and four small
counters of a particular color.
One dice.*

*The board: Draw a large rainbow
enclosing a smaller rainbow: start
with a square 26 × 26 cm
(10″ × 10″) and draw in the
vertical and horizontal center
lines. Then, below the horizontal
line but parallel to it, draw three
lines, 6, 7 and 8 cm (2⅜″, 2¾″,
3⅛″) away from the horizontal
center-line.*

*The mid-point for six color bands
of each of the two rainbows lies
3 cm (1¼″) beneath the junction of
the center-lines. Around this point
should be drawn circles with a
radius of 4.5–5–5.5–6–6.5–7–
7.5 cm (1¾, 2⅛, 2½, 2¾, 3″)
for the smaller rainbow and
9–9.5–10–10.5–11–11.5–12 cm
(3½, 3¹¹⁄₁₆, 3⅞, 4⅛, 4⅜, 4⅝, 4⅞″)
for the main rainbow. From
outside to inside the colors are:
red, orange, yellow, green, blue
and lilac. The bands end on the
two horizontal strips, which
symbolize the earth with darker
colors.*

*The smaller rainbow, which in
reality appears only occasionally
and then less clearly, shows these
colors in reverse order. Both
rainbows are larger than semi-
circles. On our large rainbow we
paint a path of water drops, 36 or
40 of which snake over the various
colors. At the highest point of the
rainbow the path is interrupted by
a vertical grey strip.*

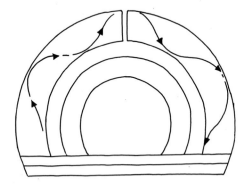

Rainbow

Rules: Start with no counters on the board.
According to the total they throw on the
dice, one after the other the players move
their counters along the left side up to the
top and down the right-hand side. Any
player who ends up on the vertical center-
line slides down the rainbow back to the
start. But a player who falls in this way for
the third time slides to the finish down the
right-hand side, gaining good luck from
misfortune.

If a counter meets another counter, owned
by the same or another player, then the
second counter must go back to the start.
Another possible rule is that players may
throw twice on the yellow, and that on the
blue strip they must go back to the last blue
raindrop. Invent your own rules. The winner
is the first player to land all his pieces back
on earth at the bottom right-hand corner.

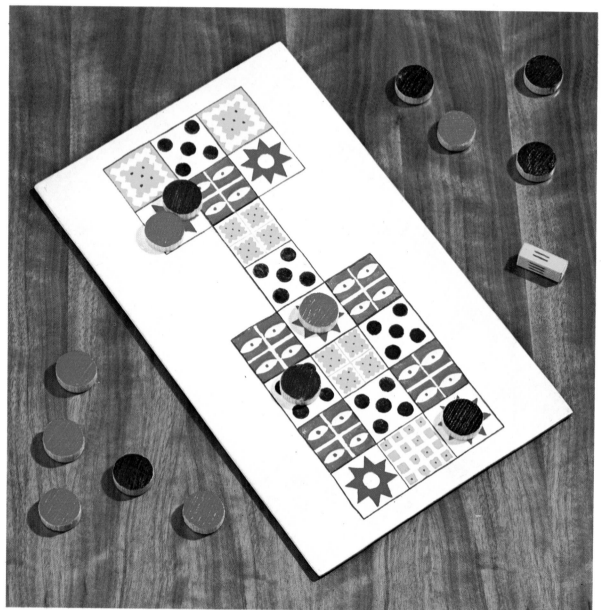

ROYAL GAME

You need: *Two players. One is given seven light-colored counters, the other seven dark counters. Here too you need a four-sided dice.*

The board: *Draw a rectangle 26.4 cm (10″) long and 9.9 cm (3¾″) wide. Divide it into 24 squares, each 3.3 × 3.3 cm (1¼″ × 1¼″). Rub out two squares on each side in the third and fourth row from the top so that only the two center squares remain to join the top 6 with the lower 12. Paint the 20 squares with themes varying in size and number, as the colorful illustration shows: five red flowers, five green double pairs of eyes, five (times five) blue dots and five yellow ones.*

PALM TREE

You need: *Two players. One is given five light-colored counters and the other five dark counters. One four-sided dice.*

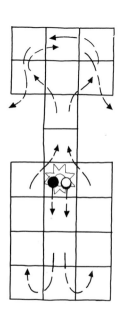

Royal game of Ur

This is a 5000-year old dice game from Mesopotamia.

Rules: Any player throwing a four, places a counter on the flower in the middle row. This piece is then moved along the middle of the twelve-square rectangle and at the bottom edge it turns right for the first player and left for the second.

The counters then move along the outside edge and over the red flower in the middle row. Then they go over the two bridging squares up to the green pairs of eyes in the

six-square rectangle. Again the first player's counter turns right, the other player's left round the outside and on reaching the red flower on the opponent's side the counter has left the playing area.

Several pieces may stand on this final red square, which provides both rest and protection from the opponent. On all other squares the piece is in danger for if met by an opponent's counter it must leave the game. Only one piece at a time may stand on the green, blue and yellow squares.

If a player is unable to make a move he must wait until the path is clear or until a

The board: *In a rectangle draw the palm tree along a center-line which lies 9 cm (3½″) from the two longer sides of the board. The trunk is 20 cm (8″) long and tapers off toward the top with angular lines running across.*

The tree-top, a circle of 2 cm (¾″) diameter, is 8 cm (3¼″) from the top of the board and it has 14 fronds. The sun hangs 4 cm (1½″) higher and is composed of circles with diameters of 1 and 2 cm (⅜″ and ¾″).

To the right and left of the sun, and curving downwards, are four small circular dots and one dot of 1 cm (⅜″) diameter in the corner. The corners should be 5.5 cm (2¼″) from the top and 3 cm (1¼″) from the side of the board.

A repeated series of four dots and a circle runs along the curved edges at the sides. Of the dots and circles leading to the treetop to the right and left of the trunk, the first and second circles at the bottom are joined with arcs, the third circles are joined with center circles on the outside with curling lines. The other outer circles have double crosses. Now paint the board.

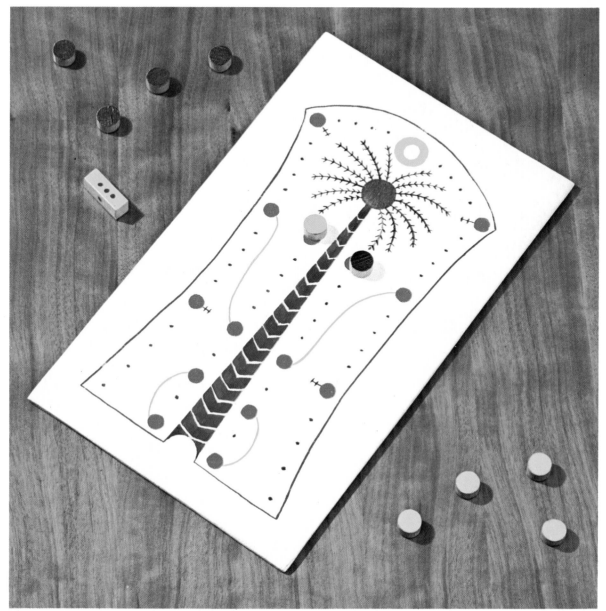

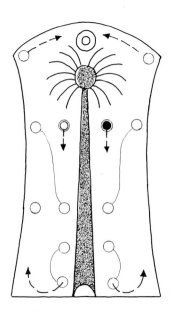

throw of the dice allows him to hop over an opponent. The piece over which he jumps must then be taken from the board and it leaves the game. A player may not hop over his own pieces. The first player to get most counters over the course is the winner.

Palm tree

This is a dice game from ancient Egypt.

Rules: When a four is thrown, a counter is placed on the topmost circle beneath the top of the palm tree. The first player starts on the right-hand side, the second player on the left. Depending on the totals thrown, counters move down the trunk, up the outside dots on the left and right, across the arc at the top, down the other side and up the opponent's side of the tree trunk.

If a counter lands on one of the circles joined with arcs or curly lines, the piece slides along this line, forwards or backwards, to the other circle. That may be an advantage or a drawback. On circles with the double cross, a player can throw the dice again. But two pieces must never stand together on the same circles. An approaching counter must

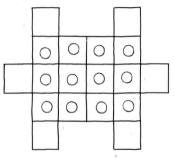

MIXED SALAD

You need: One player and a number of spectators who take their turns later. Twelve round or square counters – each of a different color.

The board: Draw a rectangle 18 cm (7½") long and 15 cm (6¼") wide divided into 30 small squares each 3 cm × 3 cm (1¼" × 1¼"). Rub out two squares at the corners and on both sides of the center two squares so that only 18 remain. The six projecting squares at the edge are finishing squares, and should be painted in a uniform gray. Color each of the remaining 12 squares differently. For each color there should be a counter in a corresponding color. The counters must be somewhat smaller than the squares so that the colors on the board are visible.

wait until the square is free or until a good throw of the dice makes it possible to hop over.

The sun above the palm tree is an exception. Here pieces belonging to both opponents may stand together, provided that the circle was reached with an exact throw. For the final circles below the treetop the players must also throw exact totals. The first player to get all five pieces under the treetop on his opponent's side wins the game.

Mixed salad

Rules: Mix the 12 pieces up and position at random on the 12 colored squares. Then, avoiding the outside squares, move the pieces back and forth until each piece stands on a square of the correct color. No hopping.

If two or more players wish to compete, the color sequence of the pieces should be written down before the game, so that every player has the same starting conditions. Then count and note down the moves. The player who makes the least number of moves wins.

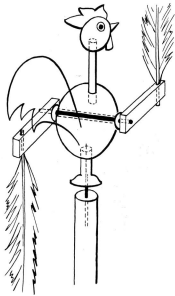

Wooden toys

You can make many attractive toys from the wide variety of wooden balls and colored wooden beads now available. This chapter should give you a few ideas for various objects: for example, amusing figures for a children's birthday party, festive decorations, small gifts for children, and puppets. You can also use small wooden pins, laths, cotton reels or spools, remnants of fur and other materials, and paints.

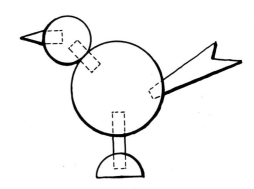

What to do

To join the separate parts (for example, the head and body of an animal), use a wooden pin or dowel. First drill a hole the width of the wooden pin in both sections. Then cut the pin off at the required length and glue it into the two parts. If you use beads or small wooden balls a very thin pin or skewer will be adequate. Depending on how thick it is, the wooden pin can function as either neck or leg. Unless you use a dowel, the figure will not hold together permanently because the areas of contact are too small. Glue beaks and legs into previously drilled holes.

As far as possible, use holes provided in the wooden balls. When you have to drill a hole yourself, always screw the ball into a vice. It need not be a large one, but you cannot do the job properly without one. To protect the wooden balls, line the clamps with folded cardboard or remnants of leather. You also need hemispheres (for example, for the feet of upright animals or for eyes). To make these, put the bead or ball on a small wooden board – a chopping board will do – with the hole facing upwards, so that the grain of the wood runs vertically. Hold a sturdy knife or chisel directly over the middle of the hole and hit it with a hammer. The wooden ball will split in two immediately.

To make birds' tails, wings and combs, saw the appropriate shape out of thin (3–4 mm: $\frac{1}{8}$") plywood with a coping saw, smoothing the edges off with a file and sandpaper. Take a fretsaw and saw slits as required, filing them until they are large enough for the parts to be inserted slightly. Drill a hole if the tail of a bird is very narrow at the point where it joins the body.

Round the end off with a file. Sometimes you can't avoid sawing the slits longer than necessary. If that happens, mix sawdust with glue and put it in the hole. When the mixture has hardened smooth it off at the edges with sandpaper. It's much easier to make tails and wings out of colored *balsa* or wood-strip, which you simply cut out and glue on. If you want curved feathers pull the *balsa* between your thumb and the blade of the scissors. It is advisable to prime the surface before

painting so that the wood doesn't absorb too much paint. Take a little paste and apply a thin coat with a brush or rag. That will fill any pores in the wood and prevent the colors running. As soon as the paste is dry, begin painting. When the object or animal is painted and thoroughly dry, finish the job by applying a protective layer of clear lacquer. If you use *acrylic paints*, that won't be necessary.

To make the cock or rooster weathervane, proceed as before. For the body take the largest wooden egg you can find, a big wooden darning-egg or a large wooden ball. The tail must be large enough for the wind to find enough resistance. For the wings you need a piece of (dowel) beading for the axis plus two pieces of lath. Drill a hole slightly larger than the beading right through the body from side to side. This hole must be just large enough for the beading to be able to turn in it easily. Then drill a hole in either end of the wooden axis, into which you glue a piece of square lath. Remember to point

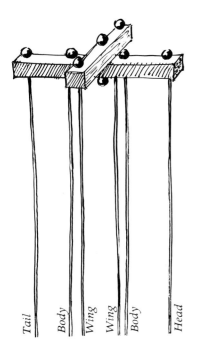

Tail   Body   Wing   Wing   Body   Head

Drill holes through each of the pieces you intend to use and string them together with nylon thread secured round small screw-eyes fixed into the body. Join each part of the animal to a nylon thread hanging from a cross made of two strips of wood which must also be free to move. For the bird's beak you can use a clothes' peg. This bird is also intended as a weathercock for your balcony or garden.

one piece of the lath upwards and the other downwards. You can also insert another small wooden bead between the body and the pieces of lath. Then drill a hole in the end of each of the pieces of lath into which you insert two large feathers, one facing forward, the other backwards.

For the foot, take a large cotton reel or spool from which you have removed one end, or even a piece of beading drilled through lengthwise. To join the foot to the body drill a hole under the body of the cock deep

enough to take a metal pin such as a large nail without its head. But don't drill through the axis as well. Then find a broom handle with a metal spike on the end on which to set the cock. For the metal spike you can take either a nail or a fairly thick metal knitting needle, provided it has a sharp point at the end. To fix it into the broom handle drill a hole in the top of exactly the same length and width. If you use a knitting needle, saw off the head. Test the length of the nail or needle before glueing it into the hole, as there should be a small gap between the foot of the cock and the broom handle.

Finally, paint the completed cock with oil paint, ending up with a coat of varnish to protect it against the weather. Attach it securely to the balcony or to a fence or roof in the garden where you can enjoy watching it turn in the wind.

If you want to suspend a bird from the ceiling, drill a hole the width of a match at the appropriate spot. Then feed the thread or string into the hole followed by a drop of glue and a small piece of matchstick to hold it in place. To perch a bird on a branch, drill a small hole underneath into which you glue a pin, head first, wedging it fast with a matchstick. Dressmaker's pins with glass heads are best for this as they do not bend easily and are very sharp. If the head is too large, break it off gently with a hammer.

Another way to hang a bird up is to suspend the thread or string from a nail or screw in the ceiling. When you have sandpapered all the parts begin painting.

Paint the stripper on with an old brush. After a short while the old paint begins to peel and it is easy to scrape it off with a spatula. If there are several layers of paint you may have to repeat the process. When you get down to the bare wood rub it over with an ammonia solution (one part ammonia to three parts water), and let it dry. When the paint is still in good condition you need only rub it down with medium sandpaper if you are going to paint over it with lacquer paint. But if you are going to use resin paint, remove all traces of old oil paint beforehand. If the wood has been waxed, clean it off with ammonia, soda or a weak solution of caustic soda. Then wash it over with plain water and let it dry.

Scratches, holes and other damaged areas can be filled with a plastic wood, or an all-purpose filler (one which dries quickly). Press the filler in tight with a spatula and leave it to dry overnight. Sand down all fillings. Use it stretched over a wooden or cork block. Remove the ensuing dust with a soft brush, cloth or vacuum cleaner.

Any furniture painting is as good as the surface you paint on. All these preparations are tiresome but absolutely essential. Try to keep your furniture absolutely level while you paint. Take off cupboard doors and lay them on wood blocks.

Lacquer paints: All lacquer paints need a white undercoat. Put it on and leave it to dry overnight.

Water paints: Give them an undercoat of poster paint; it dries much more quickly. But it is also advisable to leave this to dry overnight too.

Resin paints: An undercoat is not strictly necessary for these. But a white undercoat would still improve the final result.

You only need to sandpaper again if you are using lacquer paints. Make the surface perfectly smooth. Smooth out any paint drips and be careful to remove all dust from the sanding.

The paint must be neither too thick nor too thin. If the paint is put on too thick, it

may later peel or crack. It is most important that the first coat should be thinner than the final one. Apply the paint evenly with a broad flat brush (make sure it is of good quality). Move your arm loosely and rhythmically. If you are using lacquer paint, leave the first coat to dry overnight. In the morning lightly sand it over, and apply the second coat. Leave the first coat to dry overnight if you are using water paint. But you don't need to sand it. A second coat is not necessary if you're using resin paint. After painting clean your brush immediately, rinse it in clean water and put it away.

It is impossible to give recipes for color combinations. Every home and everyone's taste are different. Once you have painted your furniture you may want to put a decoration on it. This is not suitable for all types of furniture. Often, painting it all over with one color is sufficient. An amateur painter of decorations on furniture should use quick-drying poster or resin paints. This means you can go on working without having to stop

It takes repeated efforts to strip off ugly remains of an unsuitable decoration. Because Biedermeier chairs are usually made of polished walnut or cherry wood and not decorated, a Biedermeier pattern was excluded. The chair was painted with lavender-blue lacquer paint (a mixture of light blue, ultramarine, white and a little carmine red). A lighter shade of the same color was applied to the seat and the carving on the chair back. A folded paper pattern was cut for the chair seat and stencilled on.

for long periods to let a single color dry. These paints are sold in small containers so that it is easy to build up a good range of colors without too much expense. Acrylic paints in tubes are also suitable.

If the background is painted with lacquer paint, clean it with ammonia and lightly sand it so that the surface can take the thinner type of paint. But oily paints can be applied straight to a surface painted with a thinner type of paint (resin or water paint). If you feel confident enough you can draw the pattern straight onto the background with a soft pencil and start painting immediately. But if you have had little practice in doing this and do not feel quite sure of yourself, make a sketch on a piece of paper first, trace it and transfer it to the surface you want it to go on. Go over the drawing on the other side of the paper with a soft pencil, or – if your background is dark – use a white color stick or crayon. Tape it firmly in place round the edges (making sure it does not wrinkle), and press out the pattern with a dead ball-point pen. When you come to the actual painting use a soft brush (Nos 2–5, depending on the size of your design). Don't be too finicky and cautious in your painting. It should look fresh and alive.

Our illustrations show door designs and a Biedermeier chair. These patterns were made by folding and cutting paper. For those without much practice this is an easy way of making a pattern. Take a piece of paper the size of the surface you want to paint, fold it down the middle and cut it with scissors into a suitable pattern. When you unfold the paper you will have a symmetrical design, which is usually very difficult to draw freehand. This method also has the advantage that it enables you to experiment with shapes and colors. Cut out a number of patterns using different colored tissue paper and try them against the background. When you have finally chosen your pattern, tape it on with clear or plastic tape, and draw round it with a soft pencil. Now you are ready to start painting.

You can also use your folded paper pattern or the outline drawn from it as a stencil. Transfer it to the non-sticky side of a sheet of transparent self-adhesive film (obtainable from a stationer's), cut it out, and stick the film onto your surface. If you have a symmetrical shape make the center of the stencil correspond with the center of your painting surface. The surface must be dry and free from dust. Press the film on with a cloth and go over the cut edges with your finger nail, so that when you paint, it cannot run under the foil.

Put the second color on with a fairly dry brush. First remove the stencil, after the first color has dried. If the color has run a bit at the edges, you can go over it with a fine brush. You can get straight lines or sharp outlines by protecting the edges with tape. But if the edge still becomes blurred you can draw in the straight line with a pen and ruler. If you are painting a window frame or round any other glass in a frame, you can cover it with tape all along the line where the glass meets the wood.

Lacquer paints and most resin paints need no further treatment. But furniture painted with water paint (or poster paint) needs protection from moisture.

Matt polish: When the painting is quite dry, rub it over with colorless beeswax and polish it with a soft cloth or brush.

Shiny polish: You can get a better shine and more protection with clear lacquer. When the painting is dry, go over it with colorless shiny sealer or a clear lacquer. You can also get this lacquer in a spray. Waxing and lacquering darken the colors.

Old peasant furniture often looks too bright when it is newly painted. It has no patina. If the surface is white the new painting may look particularly hard. This is easy to correct. From some handicrafts and art-materials suppliers you can buy a special patina preparation. But you can also get a patina by rubbing your painting over evenly with umber oil paint (a small tube is enough)

The bird house was made from left-over planks. Its shape was determined by the materials available. Another floor was placed under the roof for the smaller birds. It was important that the food should neither be blown away nor get too wet. A hole was drilled exactly through the middle of both floors through which the iron pole could be passed up to the roof. Then the house could revolve. Finally it was painted with a good weatherproof paint, and the roof was decorated with flowers and a jolly bird.

on a wad of smooth cloth. After ten minutes rub it off again with a clean cloth. If the result is too dark, give it another, lighter patina.

You can also give a patina with poster paint. When your painting is dry go over it with black or brown poster paint. Leave it to dry for two to four hours and then wash it off again with water and a sponge. The darker you want your patina to be, the longer you must leave the poster paints on.

Batik on wood and paper

The use of batik on cloth is now a well-known technique. Although complete batik kits are available from handicraft suppliers, in this chapter you learn how to use the method on surfaces other than cloth, using simple materials.

You can use batik simply for decoration or to produce toys and household utensils. Once you have mastered the technique you can make very attractive designs merely with dots and lines.

All the items shown here were made with white melted candle scraps. Remove burnt candle-wicks and any sooty marks first.

Special batik wax may also be used (one-third beeswax and two-thirds paraffin). This is essential for batik work on cloth. But you will find it is cheaper and just as good to work on paper with paraffin or candle scraps. *Colors:* If you just want to experiment, watercolors from a school paintbox will do. You can also use up leftovers of fabric dyes.

A town on light-colored cardboard. Brush technique.
Colors: orange, bright red, dark red, blue-black.

But these are not as bright as wood stains.

For good color results use wood stains, but only those which must be mixed with water and not turpentine because of fire risk. You can mix the colors with each other. To start off, the colors red, blue and yellow, and possibly brown and black, are quite adequate.

Dissolve the powder in a very concentrated form (about $\frac{1}{4}$ pint—0.117 liter—of hot water to every packet of color) then thin down this concentrate to a medium and a light shade. In this way, without mixing, you get three separate color shades from one packet of stain.

Store the staining solutions in jam or preserving jars with screw tops. Mark each jar with the color. Then you won't have to keep testing to find out the shade.

In the batik process certain areas of the light-colored material – in this case paper and wood – are covered with heated wax. The wax layer is impermeable to water. When the item is being colored the color forms into drops on the wax layer. Color is applied to the rest of the surface, avoiding the waxed areas. The waxed surfaces stay the original color. After every application of color the object must be allowed to dry thoroughly. Then new areas are covered with wax. This second layer of wax fixed the first application of color. Then color is applied once more. Waxing and coloring alternate. The process ends with an application of color. Individual layers of wax remain on the material until this is completed.

Lanterns 1 and 10: Direct method with cold batik. Lantern 4: Drip method (a). Lantern 3: Drip method (b). Lantern 8: Drip method (c). Lantern 2: Pinhead method. Lanterns 5, 6, 7, 9: Brush method.

These dandelions on India paper make a fine wall decoration. Colors: yellow, bright blue, two shades of green, dark blue. Pinhead method for the seeds. Brush method for the rest of the plant.

Blossoms on India paper can be used for greetings cards. Above: colors pink, violet, green. Brush method. Center left: brush method. Colors: bright blue, yellow, green.

Mistletoe. Colors: orange, bright green and medium green, blue. Brush method.

It is best to use absorbent paper for batik. For small items writing paper will do. To design large sheets for covering folders, albums and so on, special papers are obtainable from larger paper shops and art materials suppliers. Batik on tissue paper is particularly decorative. This comes in various strengths but the thinner varieties are not recommended. Very thin tissue paper – the type used for wrapping presents – is unsuitable, as are all heavily-sized papers.

Batik on paper

Three separate processes are involved in batik work: 1. application of wax; alternating with 2. application of color; and 3. removal of wax.

Cold batik: 1. *Direct method.* Materials: clean white candle scraps, watercolors or staining solution, writing paper.

Pressing firmly, rub the candle end on the paper. You can cover the surface of the paper with broad strips or other geometric forms. Then apply the first color with a wide paintbrush.

The paint will form drops on the waxed areas. Once it is completely dry, second and third applications of wax and color may follow. The paper must dry completely between separate applications.

Batik paper may be used to make lanterns or lampshades or to cover books and notebooks. You can also use it to cover office files and card indexes.

Warm batik: The wax is melted before application. Place the sheets of paper on newspaper. You don't have to stretch them on a frame.

78

This Aquarius was cut out with a fretsaw. Colors: light green, medium green, dark green. Pinhead method. Face: brush method.

3. *Pinhead method:* Materials: paraffin or candle scraps, writing paper (tissue paper is not suitable), colors.

Technique: You need a container to melt wax, a wooden handle, or an empty ball-point pen barrel, with a glass pin-head stuck in the end. Heat the wax.

When the glass pin-head is dipped into the wax, the wax adheres and forms a tiny point when applied to the paper. This can be spread into a larger drop. From these two basic forms you can create an almost infinite number of ornamental designs.

At first, experiment with the technique (for example, by drawing rosettes or stars on cards). Pay close attention to the direction of the wax drop. To obtain an even design, keep up your initial rhythm.

4. *Brush method.* This involves applying wax with paintbrushes 8–15 mm ($\frac{3}{8}''$–$\frac{5}{8}''$) wide. These can be cut to the right size.

When you apply wax with a brush on thin paper, the wax sometimes seeps through the paper and sticks to the newspaper underneath. As long as the wax is warm the two sheets of paper can be separated easily. Raise the paper a little with one hand while you are working.

With this technique you can produce both ornamental and figurative designs. It is possible to combine the brush method with the pinhead method. Materials as for the pinhead method.

Absorbent paper is ideal if you are using a brush. But with coarse-grained paper you must choose large-scale designs. If you are practiced and confident you can start applying wax at once. But you can draw the outline with a dark soft-tip pen on white paper, lay the batik paper on top and then follow the lines which show through. If you keep the outline clear during the first waxing you can easily draw in other lines.

Avoid drawing on the batik paper as much as possible. Once pen or pencil lines have been fixed with wax they are hard to remove and look unsightly.

2. *Drip method:* Materials: white candles, watercolors or staining solution, writing paper.

Apply melted wax with a burning candle held diagonally. (*a*) Let the drops fall onto the paper either symmetrically or at random. Apply color, then drip wax again, and so on; *or* (*b*) Hold the paper diagonally and let the wax drops run, apply color, and so on; *or* (*c*) Hold the burning candle diagonally and draw lines or curves on the surface of the paper with the dripping hot wax. It is important to be quick and careful.

Applying color

Apply color to paper and wood with a broad paintbrush. Cover the work surface with a plastic or rubber mat and several layers of newspaper. After coloring, allow your batik to dry on clean newspaper. Wood stains produce very strong colors. It is a good idea to apply color with several brushes of 3–4 cm $(1–1\frac{1}{2}'')$ wide. Use one for each primary color range.

(a) Begin with the lighter shades. All later applications should be darker. (b) For good results, keep to "warm" or "cold" colors on a single piece of work (e.g., 1. yellow; 2. orange; 3. light red; 4. dark red; or 1. light blue; 2. yellow–light green; 3. dark blue or dark green).

With time you will become more experienced. But note that some color combinations are impossible with this technique: for instance, a strong red next to an equally strong green.

If a design involves several coats of colors, don't be disappointed if the work looks incomplete after the first applications. The picture will improve with each new coat.

With frequent applications some color is likely to remain on the layer of wax. To avoid ironing these marks into the material later, scrape off the top layer of colored wax with an old kitchen knife.

Then iron the batik between sheets of crêpe paper (obtainable in rolls) on a thick layer of newspaper. Change the crêpe paper frequently. Printed newspaper is not a good substitute; the ink can come off.

Batik on wood

The techniques for wood are the same as those for paper. But keep one or two additional points in mind.

1. *Wetting:* Wood grain swells with moisture and the wood surface becomes rough. To avoid this, first dampen the surface of the wood with a sponge or brush. Then, once it is dry, rub the wood with very fine sandpaper in the direction of the grain. With wood which gets very rough, repeat this treatment.

2. *Applying glue-water:* With wood batiks the wood surface retains wax. It does not soak through the material, as is the case with paper and cloth. This means that color can run under the edges of the wax and the outlines become ragged. These fine streaks of color can be just as attractive as surface cracks in cloth batik.

But if you want a sharp outline, an undercoat of glue-water mixture must be applied

Wax may be heated with a candle. Fasten an old spoon to the mouth of the jar with adhesive tape. Then melt the batik wax (especially suitable for children's work) with a candle below the spoon. Or you can remove the lid and the base of a large pickling jar and cut a "tripod" with a strong pair of old shears. A candle will do for heating. On the tripod melt the wax in a small tin in the water tank. Use an oven hot plate, a camping stove or a fondue burner and always melt the wax in the water tank, unless you have decided to use a candle. If the wax catches fire despite all precautions, never extinguish it with water but cover with a lid.

after the first wetting and sandpapering (about one tea-spoon of cold size is mixed with $\frac{1}{4}$–$\frac{1}{2}$ pint of water: 0.117–0.235 liter).

The glue-water soaks into the wood, closes the pores and stops the color running. If you mix glue and color you can paint on the wood without color running into the grain.

3. *Planning the design:* Pencil lines can leave marks on the wood. Once they are fixed with wax you can hardly remove them. It is a help to use positive and negative stencils. Draw the design on paper, cut out the out-

Rough wood objects are suitable for batik on wood, since the surface has no protective layer of wax or varnish. To make specialized objects (for example, wall coverings) ask a carpenter to cut sheets of plywood (spruce or poplar). Very angular pieces of wood are not really suitable: the diagonally-cut wood grain (end-grained wood) makes the color darker.

Musical boxes (center) decorated with the aid of a tracing. Pinhead and brush methods. Colors: bright blue, yellow, dark green. Red candlestick: pinhead method. Colors: pink, orange, dark red. First of all the white areas at the foot of the candle and at the top edge were covered with wax. Blue candlestick: brush method. Colors: light blue, light grey, dark blue.

Square board: pinhead and brush methods. Colors: pink, violet, dark red.

Box with drawers: brush method. Colors: yellow, light blue, dark green.

Small box with curved lid (center left): pinhead method. Colors: pink, violet, lilac.

line and place it on the wood instead of a direct drawing. Use the positive stencil for the outline, while the negative stencil covers the area surrounding the ornamentation inside. You can stick down the edges with wax. Apply wax in the same way as for batik on paper.

Applying color

When using transparent paints or dyes you will find that the wood surface takes the color unevenly. This is due to the hard and soft "year rings." The soft wood which grew in summer has a looser cell structure and absorbs the color more than the hard winter layers. Furthermore, color soaks readily into the cross-cut wood – the diagonally-cut wood grain. It is correspondingly darker.

(a) To color large areas evenly, dampen the wood surface with a sponge before the first color applications. Then apply color to the still damp wood.

(b) Include the edges of boxes, lids and boards which do not have a design in every application of color.

(c) Color planning: For large-scale works work out color plans on remnants of the type of wood you are using.

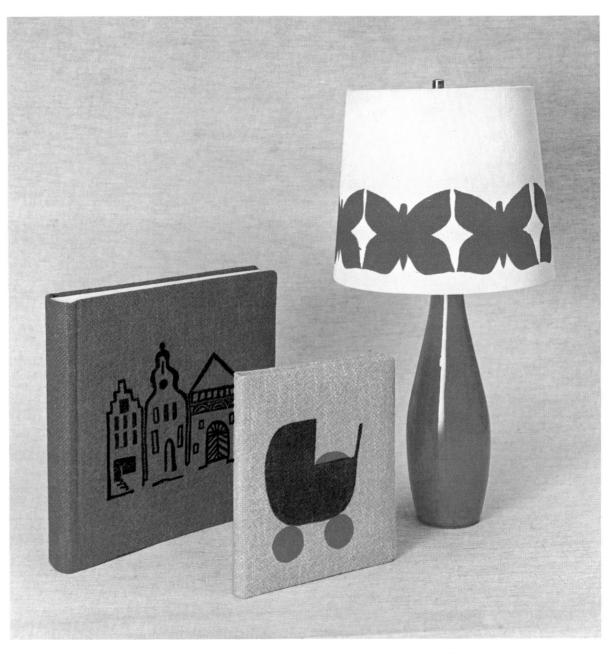

Measure the lampshade before making and marking the stencil. Here a cloth-covered album bought in a shop has been renovated with a lino-print. You can also buy and stencil a diary for your child.

Fabric printing

This chapter offers ideas for turning plain-colored fabrics into brightly-colored hand-printed articles. The use of home-made stencils and blocks can make fabric-printing an absorbing hobby.

The examples shown here were printed with color-fast fabric printing dyes available from artists' suppliers and handicrafts shops.

For white, bright and medium shades you need permanent dye; for dark materials, permanent pigment. Fabric printing dye (available in tubes) is used for blocking, and transparent dye for fabric painting. Complete instructions are usually supplied with the dyes.

The basic requirement is plain fabrics in one color, though printing can also enliven checks. Suitable fabrics are unbleached cotton, various linens, lawn, batiste, silk and georgette, though coarser fabrics such as hessian/burlap can also be used. The first job with all fabrics is to remove the size. Heavily sized white fabrics must be boiled in a solution of ordinary detergent. Place the fabrics in the cold solution, bring them to the boil, and if necessary repeat. For colored fabrics use a solution of washing soda and soap, or a detergent without a brightening agent. Don't boil delicate fabrics.

Before printing, damp-iron the fabrics. After printing, hang the finished articles up to dry.

Don't let any freshly-dyed fabric come into contact with unprinted areas. Iron the dry printed areas several times from left to right in the following weeks, as stated in the dyeing instructions. Do not wash them until at least four weeks later, and do not rub them.

Your working surface (preferably near a window) must be flat. Cover it with a soft, even material, a blanket or felt, and on top of this put one to two layers of newspaper.

Fold a piece of paper in two; draw half of a motif along the folded side, and cut it out. This is a simple fold cut, and gives a shape with two identical sides. By folding a square of paper twice or three times – the third time diagonally – and cutting a piece out of the center (the point), you can obtain more elaborate patterns. This is a central cut. Patterns for borders can be obtained by folding a strip of paper like an accordion and cutting a half shape out of the folded side.

The areas to be printed must be marked before printing. This can be done with lengths of thread or by carefully scratching very fine lines in the fabric with the point of a needle. You can also use fine pencil lines. If the material is transparent, a heavy copy of the design in soft-tip pen ink or paint can be placed under it and traced in comfort.

The Christmas stockings were made from felt. Finished dimensions: height 30 cm (12″), width of leg 17 cm (6¾″), foot length 25 cm (10″). Inner hem at top 3 cm (1¼″), seams 1 cm (⅜″). (All approximate sizes.) The red felt was printed before sewing with white paint, and a second impression was made two to three days later. For the yellow fabric, scarlet was used. Stencil. When the patterns are dry and have been ironed, double-stitch the seams on the inside. The stockings must be strong.

Then cover with blotting paper. You will need some old rags to wipe your hands.

For all printing you need a pattern. To design your own demands no great artistic skill. Most fabric printing does not require pictures, but simple geometrical or free forms, signs or symbols. These can either be distributed over the surface of the fabric or joined to form a border. When repeated they form a motif; when combined they make an attractive decoration. Another way of making a repeating pattern is by folding and cutting.

Stencilling

This technique is midway between fabric printing and fabric painting. The best material for stencils is lampshade paper, but you can use cardboard. You also need drawing paper, a pencil, a sharp knife (one with interchangeable blades), and a small pair of scissors. For printing use a stencil brush (Nos. 4–6) and fabric-printing dye.

Draw the shape on drawing paper and then transfer it to the lampshade paper. Cut out the shape and lay it on the stencil paper. Leave a border of at least 5 cm (2″) round it. Mark out the shape with dabs of color on a stencilling brush – don't put too much color on the brush – and cut out the resulting white shape with the knife. Place old newspapers underneath while you cut. When cutting, don't cut into the border, or it will let dye through in printing. The shape itself, the cut-out, must also be left undamaged. You can use both parts, the border and the shape, interchangeably for added interest.

To prevent the stencil from moving during stencilling, fix the outer rim of the "border" with adhesive tape. Secure the cut-out, and the fabric to be printed, with pins.

Do not paint with the stencilling brush in the normal way, but dab it vertically onto the fabric. Coarser fabrics need more pressure than light ones. Shake the dye well and put a very small amount in a jam jar lid. This will prevent the brush from dipping too deep.

For positive printing always begin in the center of the shape. Then work along the edge with a small quantity of bold color. For negative printing, stipple a sort of halo around the shape. If you want a more clearly defined area of color, such as a rectangle, cut out a suitable frame as a further stencil. To prevent the dye from getting under the stencil, hold the edges down during application with the fingers of your other hand.

In multi-color printing, each color requires a separate stencil. If the pattern is made up out of several shapes make a trial printing to ensure that they fit and match. A partial overlapping of shapes and colors can be very attractive. Always print the brightest color first and let it dry well before adding the next.

Some examples of blocks. 1, 2, 3: Rubber, plastic and cork stoppers of different sizes or with top and bottom used alternately. Burnish the printing surface with fine glass-paper. 4: Lino-blocks stuck on a piece of wood to make a pattern and printed in black on check. 5: Rectangles from potatoes, semi-circles from cork halves. 6: Sticking lino-blocks on cotton reels or thread spools makes printing easier. 7: Printed with a cork with a third cut off. 8: Center, a simple wooden shape. Above and below, a serrated leather edge. Dots: roofing tacks. 9: This square is printed by hand alone, and is not so bold, unlike the bolder one in (8) above, for which a mallet was used. For the lines three strands of thin wire were wound round a piece of wood at equal distances apart and colored with a brush. 10: In two colors with the upper and lower rim of a light-bulb holder. Dots with nail-heads. 11: Lino shapes, positive and negative, stuck on equal-sized pieces of wood. Impression left. 12: A right-angle of card marked out in equal sections kept the printing square. This was stuck to the cloth with adhesive tape. 13: Lino-print on hessian burlap.

To make blocks for printing, use anything from buttons and adhesive tape rolls to nail-heads and bits of glass. But you can design your own shapes. The easiest way to do this is by potato or lino cutting.

A few rules apply to all blocks. The coloring agents used are permanent color, permanent body color and fabric printing dyes from a tube. For each printing give the block a fresh coat of color, either with a brush or a pad. Make a pad by placing a piece of felt or thick woollen material in a lid and soaking it well with dye. Transfer color to lino blocks with a roller. Before each printing make sure that there is no dye on the side of the block; wipe it with a rag. Make a test run on a piece of fabric to check color tones.

Potato printing. Use a sharp knife to saw off one of the curved edges of a large, firm, raw potato. In the cut surface scratch the outline of your shape with the point of the knife. Sketch the shape in first if you wish. Then cut away the surface outside the line, leaving a slanted edge, until only the desired shape remains. Don't cut the edges too smooth. Keep them free of color. Grooves which appear in printing as unprinted lines help you to vary the basic shapes. Before printing place the cut surface on a towel to dry out, or the dye will be diluted and the edges of the shape blurred. A potato block can't be used longer than a day. After that it wrinkles.

Turnip printing and painting. A block cut from a turnip can be used for printing in the same way as a potato. But a turnip allows larger shapes to be cut.

Lino-printing. A carpet shop will provide remnants of plain 4 mm ($\frac{3}{16}$″) thick linoleum. All other supplies come from an art materials shop. All the necessary tools will be found in any cheap tool-kit. For a start you can manage with a lino knife, scraper, a special holder or an old-fashioned pen-holder.

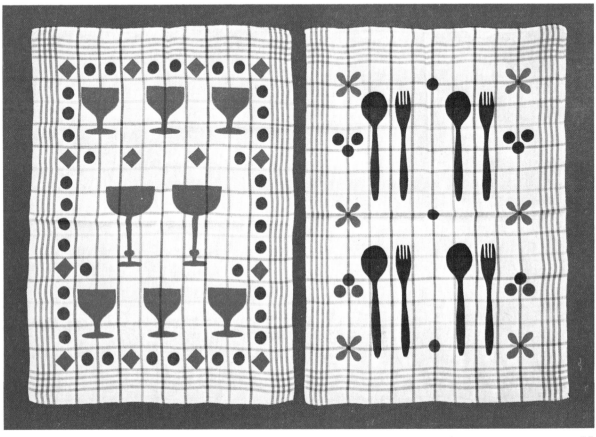

Many housewives will be pleased to have glass cloths decorated with stencils. The bright red and mid-blue dyes can be boiled. The patterns were made with folded paper. Both sides of the cloths must be printed so that the patterns coincide exactly. Boil out the size before printing.

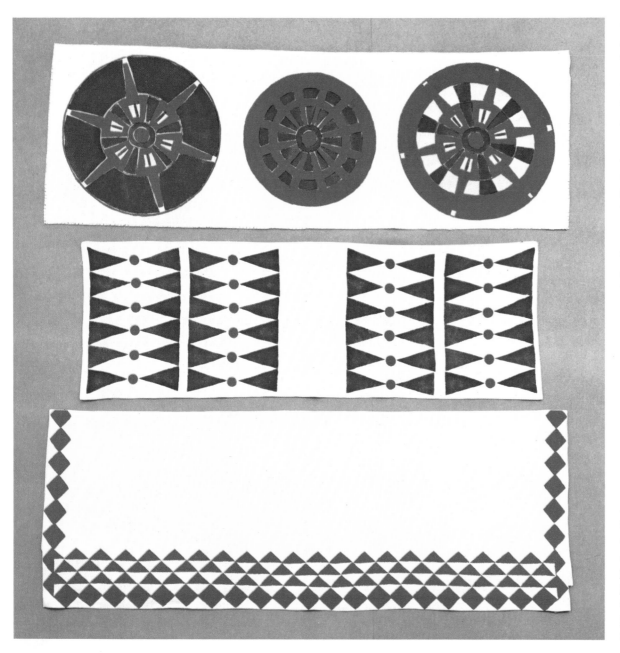

You also need an ink roller, a small sheet of plate glass, a tube of fabric-printing ink and a lino-cutting knife or blades, or sharp pen-knife or multi-blade knife for cutting the block out of the lino.

Brush the lino with a solution of warm detergent in order to remove the surface grease. After transferring the shape to the lino in the same way as for the stencil, go round it with the knife. For positive printing gouge out the background of the motif. For a negative print, groove the motif and leave the background. Remove remaining unevenness after the test printing. When cutting, always work away from yourself and press the lino firmly onto the working surface with your other hand.

Glue the finished lino block to a piece of wood which you can hold conveniently in your hand. For round shapes, empty cotton reels or spools are excellent. Glue large blocks (for which hand pressure is insufficient) to 4–5 mm ($1\frac{1}{2}''$–$2''$) plywood. Squeeze some of the ink from the tube onto

the glass and spread it evenly with the knife. Now roll the color-roller back and forth across the glass until it is evenly coated with ink. The color can then be transferred with the same backwards and forwards movement of the roller to the block. All the raised areas will receive a coating of color (offset). Now printing can start.

Greater force can be exerted standing than sitting. If hand-pressure is insufficient, use your fist or a mallet. For large blocks a rolling-pin may be useful. Alternatively, printing can be done on the floor, using your feet; that is, with your full body weight. Spread stiff ink on the glass with the help of a drop of pure turpentine.

Polystyrene is a quite light packing material for instruments and delicate objects. It makes blocks which take ink well, leave a clear impression and are long-lasting.

The best results are produced by hand-printing on fabrics of one color, though very attractive borders and patterns can also be produced on checks.

Whichever technique is used, success comes from clean and precise application of the chosen pattern. To see the effect without doing any printing at all, cut rectangles from a material such as red tissue-paper in the same size as the white diamonds and make a test-pattern with them.

A pretty border for table-napkins or blankets is not always cheap. When shopping why not keep an eye open for ribbon that could be turned into colored edging by printing? Linen and tape are available in many colors and widths. The examples shown here give an idea of the attractive results which are possible.

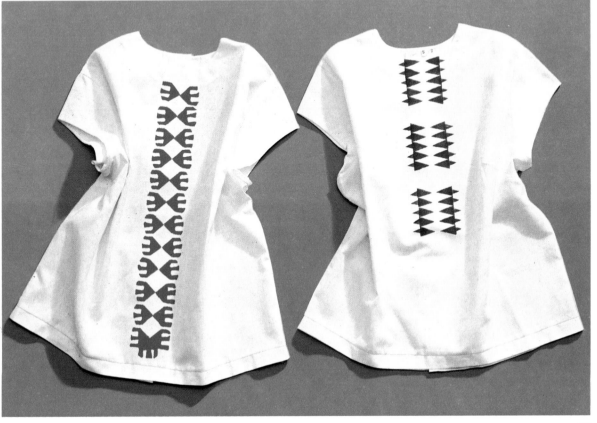

Two shirts decorated with a potato print. Colors scarlet and mid-blue. A sleeve-board was used as a support during printing.

In this chapter we offer encouragement and advice for anyone interested in lino-printing. Once you've acquired the basic technique, even multi-colored lino-cuts are not so complicated as they seem at first. You will find adequate instructions and ideas here for whatever you want to print – a book-plate, a birthday card, a wedding announcement, the title-page of a school newspaper, even a small poster.

Lino-cutting

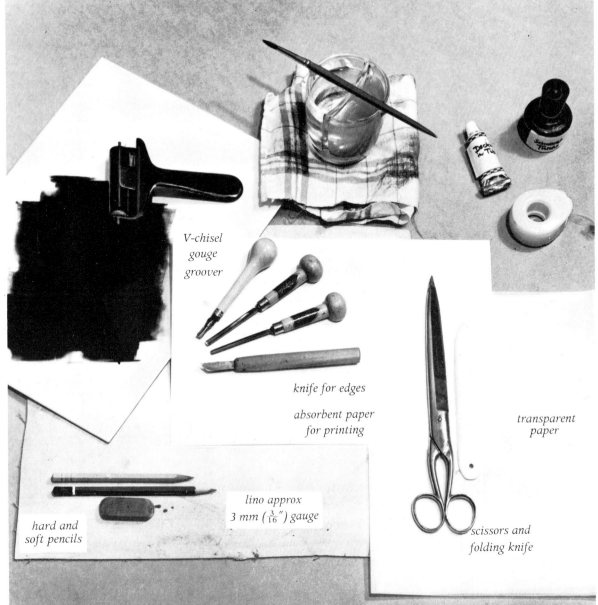

V-chisel
gouge
groover

knife for edges

absorbent paper
for printing

transparent
paper

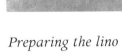

lino approx
3 mm ($\frac{3}{16}$″) gauge

hard and
soft pencils

scissors and
folding knife

Linoleum was invented in the mid-nineteenth century. It consisted of a paste made from cork-flour or wood-flour with the addition of lead oxide and resin, applied to a jute canvas backing and allowed to harden. It soon became a popular material for the production of stencils among professional artists as well as amateurs. Since lino can be easily cut or carved with a penknife even children can make simple lino-cuts and prints.

Preparing the lino

1. The lino must be 3 mm ($\frac{3}{16}$″) gauge or thicker. Don't pierce the textile backing during preparation. The lino must have a smooth surface, without grain.
2. When drawing the pattern onto the lino, take care that the shape, especially if it includes letters, appears in reverse. With symmetrical designs this does not apply.
3. Before you can draw the design onto the lino, remove all grease from the surface. Wash it with soap or detergent so that the pencil or ink will take.
4. With very dark lino, you can also rub the surface with heavily thinned "permanent white." This makes a pencil drawing stand out clearly.
5. Start with quite simple designs and small formats.
6. Use good tools which are comfortable to handle. There are various makes, at different prices, all obtainable from art materials suppliers.

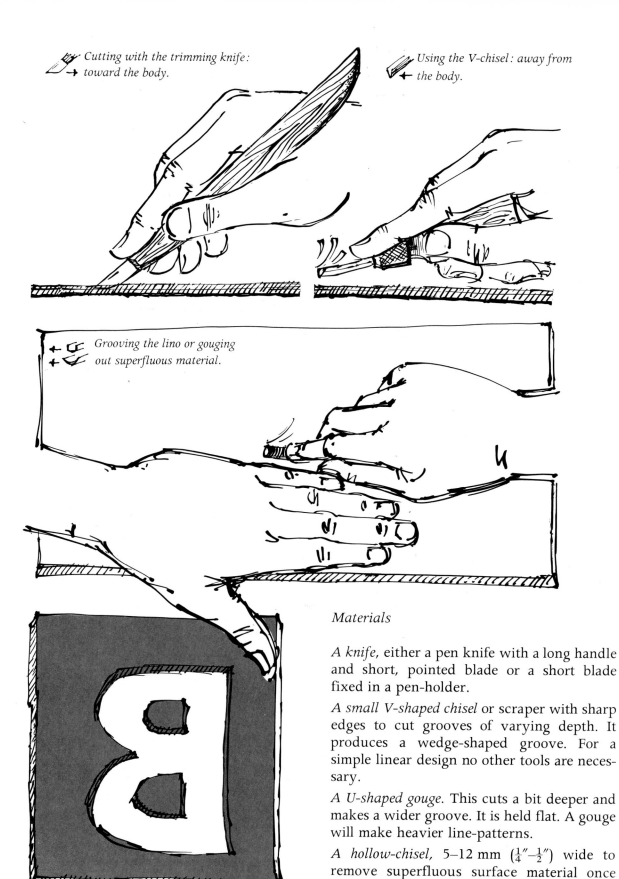

Cutting with the trimming knife: toward the body.

Using the V-chisel: away from the body.

Grooving the lino or gouging out superfluous material.

Materials

A knife, either a pen knife with a long handle and short, pointed blade or a short blade fixed in a pen-holder.

A small V-shaped chisel or scraper with sharp edges to cut grooves of varying depth. It produces a wedge-shaped groove. For a simple linear design no other tools are necessary.

A U-shaped gouge. This cuts a bit deeper and makes a wider groove. It is held flat. A gouge will make heavier line-patterns.

A hollow-chisel, 5–12 mm $(\frac{1}{4}''-\frac{1}{2}'')$ wide to remove superfluous surface material once the outline of the design has been drawn.

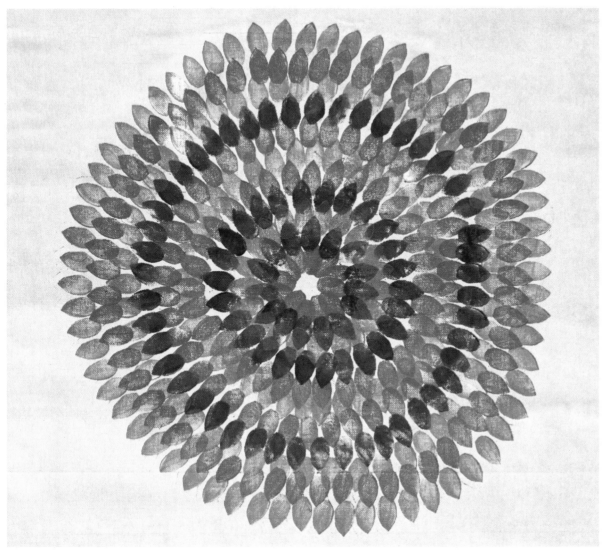

A large design in several colors produced from a small tear-shaped lino-block. Fabric dyes were used for the printing and the design printed as a decoration on linen. Glue small lino-blocks on small blocks of wood and take the ink directly from the lino block. Use it like an ink pad.

When cutting the lino, take care that deep cuts do not produce "under-cuts" or blurs. The edge of the cut should be slightly tapered.

The hollow chisel cuts away everything not needed in the print. (You can usually get all these tools, ready-made in a simple lino-cutting set.)

A sheet of glass or plastic for rolling the ink on.

Paper. White and not too thin. It should be somewhat porous to allow the color to penetrate.

A rubber roller to apply the color.

Watercolors for lino-printing. These can be bought in individual tubes or in sets of six or twelve colors.

Lino-printing inks. These are not water-soluble, and are the kind used for book-printing. A special ink remover will be needed to clean the roller, lino and glass.

A strong comb. When the paper has been pressed onto the inked printing block rub it carefully with the comb. This strengthens the impression and makes the color come off with the paper. The comb replaces a printing press: in lino-printing finger-pressure is enough to transfer the impression. For very fine lino-cuts use your thumb-nail instead.

To be suitable for printing, papers should be soft and absorbent. Japanese vellum and sized paper give particularly good results.

Cutting the lino

Put one hand on the lino with your forearm parallel to your body. Place the other hand on the fingers of the first, and with it draw the knife first left along the outline of the design.

1. A small amount of ink is squeezed from the tube onto a piece of glass or plastic.

2. The color is spread thinly and evenly with a rubber roller until the roller makes a "smacking" sound.

Then turn the lino and cut at right angles. When gouging or grooving, always direct tools *away from yourself.* The little finger of the first hand acts as a guiderail or, when necessary, as a brake.

When printing with the cut-out, first make a "proof" to see that nothing has been forgotten and that no extra bits of lino have been left which will show in the print.

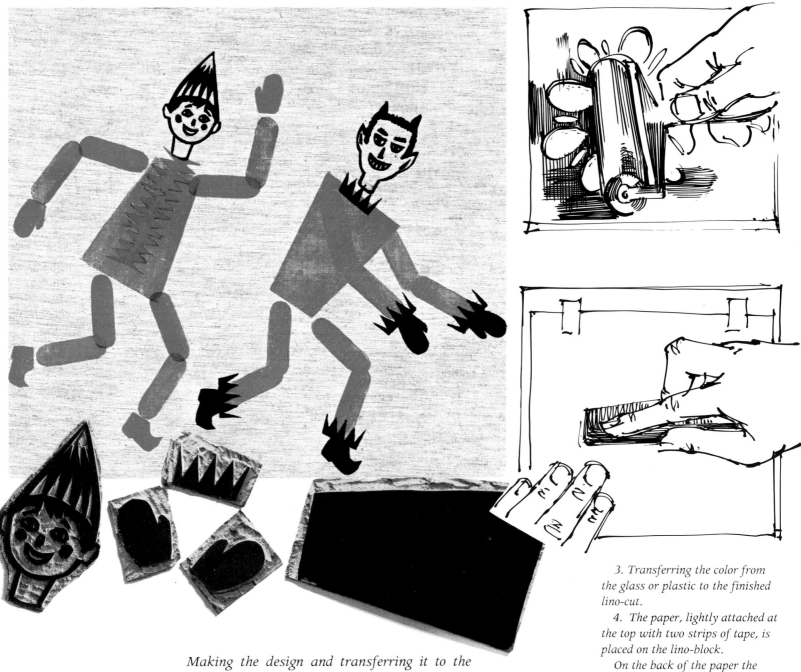

3. *Transferring the color from the glass or plastic to the finished lino-cut.*

4. *The paper, lightly attached at the top with two strips of tape, is placed on the lino-block.*

On the back of the paper the back of the comb is rubbed evenly all over the design.

Making the design and transferring it to the lino-block

The best way to begin is to make the chosen design on transparent paper (tracing paper or greaseproof paper). You can buy it in A4 size pads, or in single sheets in larger sizes.

1. The paper should be cut to the same size as the piece of lino. Even better, the lino can be cut to the same size as the design and the paper left a little larger and

93

attached with adhesive tape. You can draw the design with a soft pencil.

2. Now place a piece of carbon paper, shiny side down, between the transparent paper and the lino. You must place the drawing back to front on the lino.

3. For tracing use a hard pencil or a ballpoint pen. As you draw round the outlines of the design the shape is transferred to the lino. The design will come out even better if the lino has previously been degreased.

4. The carbon paper can now be removed, and the transparent paper taken off. To prevent mistakes in cutting and gouging, fill in the areas to be retained for printing with black paint or permanent color. With dark lino, first paint the whole surface with thinned permanent white so that the lines of the tracing show up clearly.

There are two basic rules for two or more color printing: one color to a block and all blocks the same size. Draw the areas corresponding to each color on separate sheets of transparent paper, for example, one each for blue, red and yellow. To produce secondary colors, two primary colors must be superimposed: for example, for green, yellow and blue, and for orange, yellow and red.

To avoid white edges between colors each color should overlap the others a little. When color printing, cut out a cardboard frame with the space in the middle exactly equal to the lino-plate. Then mark the transparent sheets with a small register-cross (+) to show where colors meet. Advanced printers should then have no serious problems in making colored lino-cuts.

The paper to be printed should be stuck down with its upper surface to the lino. Take

How a colored lino-cut is produced

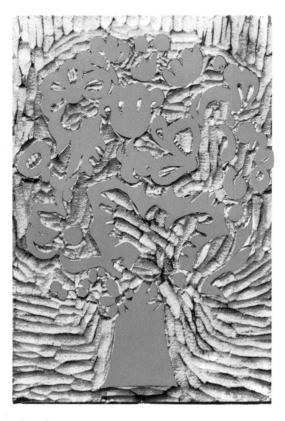

Blue plate

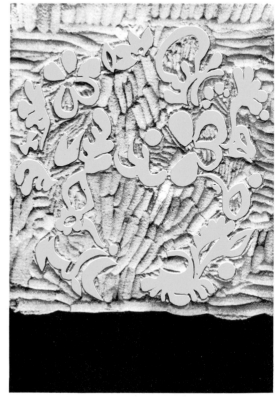

Yellow plate

94

care that it doesn't move, and that it can be lifted at any time to see how the impression is going. This means that by varying the pressure on the reverse of the paper different color shades can be applied and artistic effects attempted.

To prevent the paper from moving during printing, leave the lino a little larger at the top or sides so that you can stick the paper down on one side with adhesive tape.

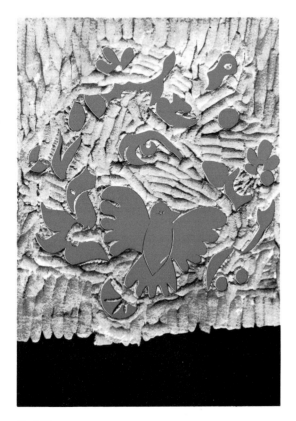

Red Plate

Composite impression

A "color section" was made for each of the three primary colors. Each color was traced onto a separate piece of lino and cut out. Since blue and yellow printed together produce green, these two plates had to be superimposed for "green". In the same way, all the red areas were combined on the "red" plate and all areas which would not print red were cut out. The result, without the use of black color, was a fine design in four colors.

One of the most interesting features of the recent revival of old handicrafts has been an interest in the decoration of Easter eggs with the simple to ornate patterns, and derivations from them, found in various parts of Europe. These eggs are excellent Easter gifts, entertain children and adults, and make charming and colorful decorations.

Easter eggs

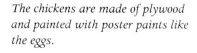

The chickens are made of plywood and painted with poster paints like the eggs.

It is a good plan to save blown eggs throughout the year and build up a stock of them. Of course you can also paint hard-boiled eggs as long as the shells are not cracked.

But in the long run, blown eggs are easier to keep than boiled ones. They also have the advantage of being easier to use for decorations. They can be hung up, threaded or glued onto all kinds of pictures.

First blow your eggs out of their shells. That is easier to do if they are at room temperature than if you take them straight out

of the refrigerator (ice-box). Don't use a needle, although that is often recommended. Use the pointed end of a strong pair of scissors. At each end of the egg carefully make a hole about 2–3 mm ($\frac{1}{16}$″) in diameter. Push in a tooth-pick and stir the egg inside so that you can blow it out more easily. Blow hard and out it comes. If you want the hole to be circular, first make a tiny opening with the scissor point and then finish off with gentle pressure from a cross-headed screwdriver (or electrical screwdriver). Wash out the eggshell thoroughly with hot water and

a little vinegar. Have you got a school paint-box in the house, or a set of water- or gouache colors? If not, get one with twelve colors: it's well worth it. Poster paints in small tins or jars also offer many possibilities. You can build up a collection of paints; even two, three or four colors give quite a lot of scope.

The traditional color for Easter eggs is red: the color of love, joy, fertility, life and resurrection. Spring-green, yellow and orange go well with it. Eggs with a velvet-black background also look most impressive.

Now you can paint your first egg. Put it on the table in front of you and place beside it a book of the same height to support your hand. Have ready your paints and a jar of water. Take a fine brush (marten hair Nos. 00–1) and paint a thin circle round the middle of the egg.

Where is the middle? Judge it with your eye but err on the side of too high rather than too low, particularly if the egg is to be hung up. Now paint a wreath of small dots round the circle. Next time round paint a leaf shape or a small blob like a tear drop. Fit the colors and shapes into one another. It won't be long

You can use poster paints on white eggs in exactly the same way as you use water paints. One advantage is that these paints are water-resistant and you don't need to use lacquer. Neither do they bleach in the sun. They are only damaged by greasy fingers. Another advantage is that you can paint one poster color over another. This means that you can paint the background in one color and the pattern on top of it in other colors.

before you have finished decorating your circle. If you like, you can do another one on the back of the egg. But you can also leave it plain or write the year and Happy Easter on it.

If you feel nervous about painting straight onto the egg, draw your pattern on it in pencil first. You can even rub it out if you don't press too hard.

If the paint doesn't stick to the egg properly, there are probably traces of grease on it. Rub the shell with vinegar or a scouring powder. If your fingers are warm and moist the colors may run. So be careful. It is a good idea to spray the finished egg lightly with lacquer.

Get some straws of different thicknesses. One is sure to fit. Push it through the holes of your egg until it goes easily. Take some poster paint from a tin and put it on newspaper or an old plate and thin it with a little water. Using a thick paintbrush, quickly paint stripes on the egg from top to bottom. Do not let the paint run or streak, or gather

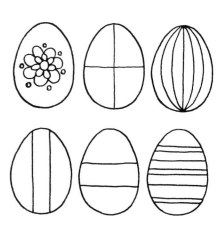

98

in drops. When you have done this, look to see how the paint is holding. Poster paints are thicker than water paints and dry quickly. You may get hard edges you do not want. The faster you work the better the result. If you don't want to paint your egg at random – with dots or an Easter rabbit in a field, for example – note that the shape of the egg requires certain precise divisions to make it ornamental. You can go for two corresponding sides; four quarters, eight eighths, equal longitudinal divisions, a broad vertical or horizontal stripe, or rings round the egg.

You can also combine your egg-decorating with another hobby. Use snippets of colored tissue paper (or cut it folded), dried flowers, wool, bits of lace or braid, beads, wax or straw.

It's quite easy to draw on the egg with a pen-holder and a fine nib. But black Indian ink will run if the egg shell is not completely free of grease. These patterns look particularly good on snow-white or dark brown

eggs. The spaces in between can be partly filled in with black. A sparing application of white water or poster paint is also very effective. You can add more color. Spray the eggs lightly with lacquer.

You can also use fibertip pens. Cover white eggs with white poster paint. This thin layer ensures that the color of the felt pen takes and dries matt. You can write on an egg with a soft-tip pen. Even ballpoint pens can be used without smudging. But children like using soft-tip pens. Perhaps you can do the white background for them beforehand.

plate. You have already hard-boiled your eggs with onion skins or a special egg dye. You need only a wooden pen holder and a drawing nib. Dip it in the acid and draw a pattern on the egg. If the acid fizzes too much, throw some away and carefully thin out your solution. Leave the acid on the egg for a little time to work in; meanwhile go on drawing. Then wipe it with a paper handkerchief and finally run it over, so that the drawing comes out clearly. You may have to go over some places. Lightly oil the finished egg.

Scratching technique

Etching on colored eggs with hydrochloric acid is not dangerous if you make sure that the acid doesn't come into contact with any broken skin, doesn't fall on clothes, and isn't disposed of in metal containers, but down the lavatory. *But don't let children try this technique!*

Half fill a brandy glass with water and add a little hydrochloric acid so that you have two parts water to one of acid. Stir it with a wooden stick. Put the glass carefully on a

Although you can use blown eggs for the above techniques, when you first try the scratching technique, stick to hard-boiled ones. Avoid eggs with bumps on the shell.

The following tools are recommended: sharp pointed three-cornered file, knife, nail, penknife, razor blade, can opener.

Stain the egg with strong coloring. Scratch a pattern on the eggshell with a sharp instrument. Begin scratching with care. It is best to start by marking out divisions on the egg and then to develop ornamental shapes from these divisions. The scratched patterns often look like lacework. The technique requires patience and a steady hand. One egg can take hours.

Another possibility is to use wax colors. If the egg is still warm you can rub on various colors (going from light to dark). It is easy to scrape the colors to the right shade with a palette knife. Wax colors are much easier to remove than colors obtained from egg or fabric dyes. Wax colors stick to the upper layer of the eggshell whereas egg or fabric dyes sink in further. When you want to scrape an egg to which wax colors have been applied, hold it in your lap because warm hands cause the wax to melt and smudge. The pattern on the eggshell can be set by rubbing on floor wax or lacquer.

Another variation of the scratching technique is to use a knitting needle for dipping a blown egg in melted wax to which beeswax has been added to make it more malleable. Then scratch or cut (according to the thickness of the wax layer) a pattern with a sharp

instrument. The egg can also be colored beforehand in a suitable color. Have something ready to hang it up with before you dip the egg in the wax.

Potato prints

Draw a pattern and cut it on the potato for the children beforehand. Put paint on a glass plate and let the children get on with the

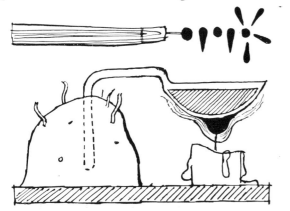

printing. The potato print should not be more than about 1 cm ($\frac{3}{8}$″) in diameter, or it won't fit onto the rounded surface of the egg. Instead of potato prints you can use spruce twigs, moss, and so forth.

Wax blocking (Batik)

Materials:

Various sized needles stuck into small bits of wood or pencils.

Goose-feathers whose points have been cut into various geometrical shapes.

Potato halves.

Old bent tea spoons.

Candle or spirit (alcohol) lamp.

Batik wax or beeswax mixed with 50 per cent stearin (candle wax).

Tins with prepared egg or fabric dyes.

Put the wax in the spoon and heat it. Don't let it boil. Take a needle, dip the head into the wax and quickly transfer it to the

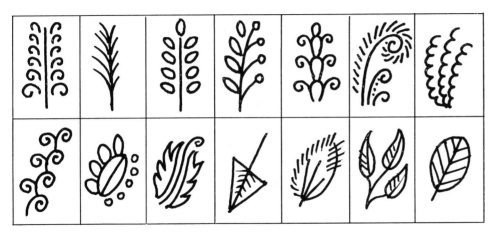

Eggs made by Heidi Haupt-Battaglia of Berne.

egg, making a single dot. Dip the needle into the wax to make each further dot or teardrop shape. You can get a pleasing pattern by making rows of dots, drops and squares. A needle and a feather in turn can be used to decorate the same egg.

When you have finished the wax pattern, put the egg into the prepared warm dye solution. Be careful that the temperature is not above 40° C (104° F) or the wax will melt. On the other hand, a cold dye solution colors unevenly. You can use a spoon to douse the egg with dye several times so that the color takes evenly. When it is the color you want, take the egg out carefully and dry it with a soft cloth (which you must always have by you to stop the egg rolling away). If the color has taken evenly, you can start to melt off the wax. Do this either with the edge of a candle flame (the top smokes) or over a gas or spirit lamp. Wipe off the soft wax with a soft absorbent cloth. On no account scratch the wax off. Now you can see the white wax design standing out against the colored ground.

If you want the egg to have more than one color, leave on the first wax coating and when the egg is dry from the first coloring add another wax design. Then color it again in a darker color. This can be repeated for up to five colors. You have to take care (as in batik) to apply the colors in the right order. Go from light to dark from white (eggshell), to yellow, orange, light red, dark red, blue, purple or black. Leave all the wax on till you have finished the final coloring.

Begin from the top hole and cover the egg with a net pattern. Only use pencil where you will paint over it later. So be careful with it. If you want to divide the egg into equal parts there is a simple trick. Cut a narrow strip of paper and put it round the egg, cut it off where it meets. Fold this "cummerbund" once or more according to your plan and mark in pencil where the folds come on the egg. If you want to find the exact middle of the egg, put another strip of paper round it from top to bottom. Of course this only works if the holes at the top and bottom are centrally positioned. Develop your pattern outwards from the pencil marks and let it spread. It's always better to develop the pattern as you go along than to work it all out too precisely in advance. A paper sketch is inadequate because it can't take the egg's roundness into account.

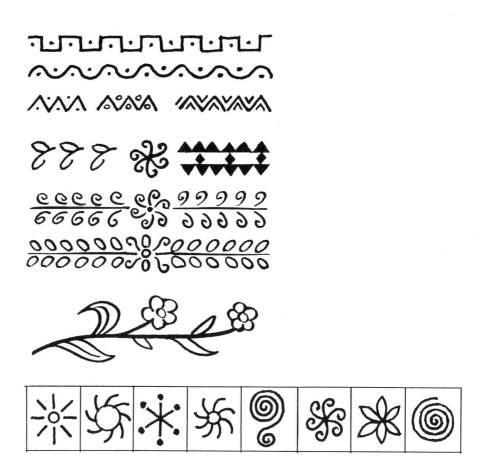

Elements of egg decoration

Perhaps decorating eggs arose from human beings' perennial need to be creative and to give well-loved, every-day things a festive appearance beyond the necessities of common use. It seems likely that decorated eggs were originally symbols of salvation, or pledges offered by human beings not yet accustomed to speaking much. In fact we can find such ideas in the egg-decoration patterns of many nations. You should perhaps try to find a meaningful pattern for your Easter eggs. There are three kinds of pattern: the geometric or abstract; the stylized; and the naturalistic.

Let children help you prepare for a festival. They can express their ideas in their own way.

The picture shows eggs decorated by wax blocking from Moravia (Czechoslovakia). The writing tool used is called a "stuzka," a

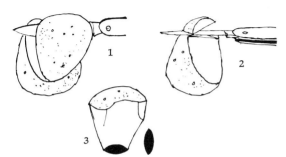

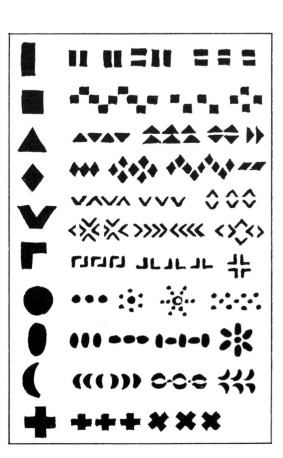

"What shall I paint on the egg? I've no idea!" people often say. Two bits of advice: Don't be over-ambitious; go carefully at first. The most attractive patterns can be made up of dots of different sizes and the tear-drop shape. Don't get bewildered by a finished design, simply go step-by-step. Open your eyes and look at the patterns on carpets, your friends' dresses or ties. These patterns were all created by designers and you can copy or adapt them.

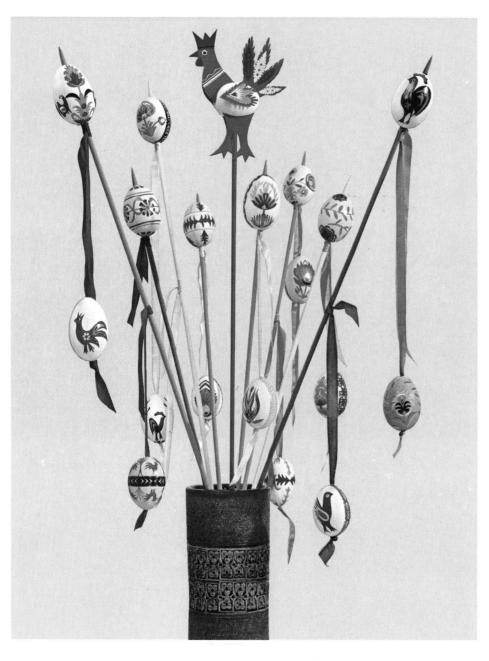

strong small reed of about a millimeter ($\frac{1}{16}$″) set in a wooden handle.

You can also use a feather quill. This is a little more difficult but you can try it beforehand on paper or old eggshells.

The egg bouquet is easy to make and is joyful and bright.

Get some small round wooden sticks about 6 mm ($\frac{1}{4}$″) in diameter from a woodwork shop or timber/lumber yard and cut them to various lengths. Sharpen them a bit at each end and paint them. Tie colored ribbons at one end and stick the decorated egg on the other with a little glue at the joint. A small piece of cardboard will prevent it slipping. Eggs whose holes have become too big can be stuffed with a flower shape made from colored paper. You can also slide eggs onto the colored ribbons. A knot or bow under the egg will stop it sliding down.

Then fill a pot or a vase with sand, peat or earth and push in the sticks, arranging them to form a bouquet.

You can add an Easter note by forming two of the sticks as a cross (you will have to shorten one of them).

A small table decoration is quickly made by fixing an egg-stick into a halved wooden ball (perhaps from a curtain rail or rod). Or you could use the top of a cotton reel or spool; cut, and rounded off with a file, it makes a good base for a table decoration.

These egg flowers were made from thin plywood, small wooden sticks and beads.

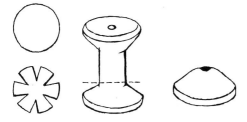

Rosette made of shiny or flat paper.

Cotton-reel or spool base for table decoration.

The Easter tree

Make the tree out of square or round wooden poles. The central trunk is about 70 cm (27½″) long. Either the vertical or the cross-pieces are slightly bent at the joints and nailed together or tied with garden twine. Drape this framework with greenery and tie firmly. Begin with the cross-pieces and work inwards, and finish with the vertical, working from top to bottom. Put the tree into a pot you have ready, or better still into a flower pot with green shoots growing in it. You can also cover the pot with moss, and stick fresh spring flowers into it. Now hang the two colored eggs on the cross pieces. The eggs could show symbols of the Church year or Easter symbols.

How can you get a pot of young green grass? Fill the pot at least half way up with sand and then add a layer of well-moistened peat, garden soil or sawdust. Then sow thickly already germinated grass seed, barley, oats or cress. Cover the seed with a thin layer of earth or peat. Keep the pot warm and always moist. The seeds should come up in about 6 to 8 days. Children (especially if they live in cities) are delighted to see the seeds coming up.

Allow the seeds to germinate for a day or two in a pot filled with warm water. Keep adding warm water till the seeds begin to open.

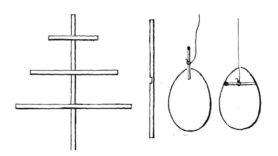

This Easter tree will capture many hearts.

In the middle of the street and on both sides of the river stands the tree of life. It bears twelve fruits; each month brings its own fruit.

The Easter tree represents the tree of life.

107

Board games consist of numerous small pieces which can be combined in endless different variations. They are similar to jigsaw puzzles, except that instead of composing one picture following a prescribed design, you get different formations whenever you lay out the pieces.

These games not only test your patience but your skill in combining different elements. They stimulate your imagination and train your sense of color and form. They are creative games.

To make the small games you need very little material. For the cat use colored cardboard or thick white drawing paper. If you have a drawing board, rule and square, so much the better. To cut out your shapes, fix the paper or cardboard on which you have drawn the outline onto a firm base such as stiff cardboard or glass. Then cut along a ruler or square. Make sure you cut accurately, otherwise the pieces of the game will not fit together properly.

Match-box games

Games on a larger scale. You can, of course, make all these games on a larger scale, but do remember to use a stronger quality paper or cardboard. Learning how to cut thick cardboard precisely takes some practice. Scratch a line along the ruler (a metal one is best for this) and continue cutting, pressing hard while doing so. Alternatively, you can al-

ways have the cards cut for you by a bookbinder or printer, especially when you need a large number. If you prefer working with wood, use plywood approximately 4 mm ($\frac{1}{4}''$) thick. Cut out the individual pieces with a wood saw and smooth the edges off with sandpaper. If you want to paint the wood, use emulsion paint as it dries fast, is waterproof and will not chip easily. If you are using non-fast colors, allow them to dry and then give them a coat of wax or varnish.

The Chinese patience game is a real brainteaser for all the family. Like many other games it originated in China and is over 2000 years old. Using the seven sections of the oblong (see diagram) you can make an endless variety of shapes. But you must always use all seven pieces – this is often more difficult than you might think.

The pieces are simple to make and do not require much material. *You will need:* two matchboxes, white cardboard 3.5 cm × 7 cm ($1\frac{3}{8}'' × 2\frac{3}{4}''$), about 10 to 15 cards 3 cm × 4 cm ($1\frac{1}{4}'' × 1\frac{5}{8}''$) and red and blue adhesive foil. *What to do:* Glue two matchboxes together lengthwise and cover with a strip of blue foil 5.2 cm × 12 cm ($2'' × 4\frac{3}{4}''$). Then cover the piece of cardboard with a strip of red foil measuring 6.5 cm × 8.5 cm ($2\frac{1}{2}'' × 3\frac{3}{8}''$), and glue the edges firmly to the back. You are then ready to glue the

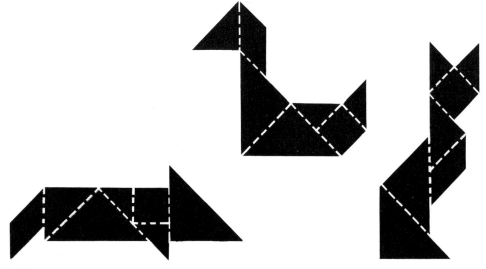

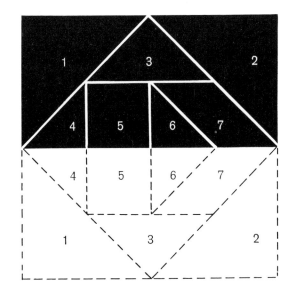

covered cardboard to the boxes. Cover one side with red, the other with blue. Fill in the cards on which the pieces are to be placed as in the sketch. They should measure 3.5 cm × 7 cm ($1\frac{3}{8}'' \times 2\frac{3}{4}''$). The dotted lines are only necessary when you are making two games simultaneously. Cover the backs and the seven pieces with blue or red self-adhesive foil. Alternatively, you can use colored cardboard or paint it yourself. If you are using thin drawing paper, take a piece 7 cm square ($2\frac{3}{4}''$) folded down the middle

and glued together. Then cut out the seven pieces.

Society game. Paint each player's set of seven pieces a different color. When several people are playing at the same time it is advisable to use a larger format, for example, 6 cm × 12 cm ($2\frac{1}{2}'' \times 5''$). Another suggestion is to draw in only the contours onto the cards, perhaps inserting the dotted lines on just one or two of the sections. *How to play:* Place the card in the middle. The players must then

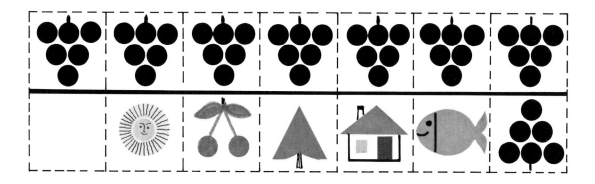

try to reproduce the sample pattern as quickly as possible. The first to succeed is the winner. To prevent cheating, each player should stand an open book in front of his card. To make the game more appealing to small children, use two different colors on the card. The case is made from a larger box. Divide it into two parts, one for the sample cards and one for the small pieces.

Picture dominoes is a very old game, said to have been invented by a certain Abbé Domino. Our game is organized according to the classical system of point dominoes. Dominoes consists of 28 cards ranging in value from 0 to 6, each number appearing once doubled and once with every other number. You are free to increase the number of cards. Hence if you use the numbers 0 to 7, you will have 36 cards; 0 to 8, 45 cards; and 0 to 9, 55 cards. Dominoes is played by laying the cards out in succession on the table, so that each card is followed by one that corresponds to it either in terms of number, color, shape or number of images. For the domino game illustrated here the format chosen was 4 cm × 8 cm ($1\frac{1}{2}''$ × 3''). Cards of this size fit in a suitable packet which

you can cover with self-adhesive or clear foil. *You need:* 28 cards, 4 cm × 8 cm ($1\frac{1}{2}''$ × 3''), made of white drawing board; a black ball-point pen, six different colored soft-tipped pens; and some self-adhesive transparent foil.

What to do: Trace your motif onto the prepared cards using carbon paper. Sketch in the outlines firmly with a black ball-point pen and paint each number a different color. Each number should have the equivalent number of motifs, so for example the number five will have five balloons, five cups or five apples, and so on. The numbers two, four and five are coupled with zero. You can leave the numbers out, but they are useful as "dice" in the game. The motifs shown here are really only intended as suggestions. It is far more original if you and your children draw and paint your own motifs. The children will be proud of their home-made game, and it also makes a most attractive present. It is advisable to cover the cards with self-adhesive transparent foil.

How to play: This is a group game for two to six players. With six players each takes 4 cards, leaving 4 over. With five players each

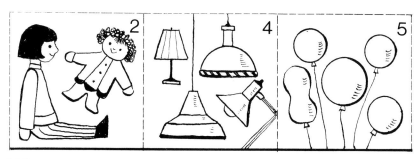

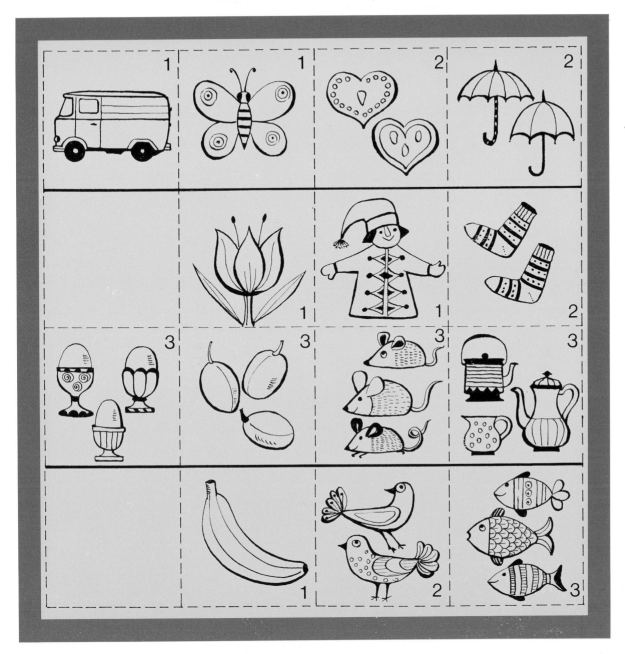

takes 5 cards, leaving 3 over. With four players each takes 6 cards, leaving 4 over. With three players, each takes 8 cards, leaving 4 over. With two players each takes 8 cards, leaving 12 over. Shuffle the cards and deal according to the number of players. The remainder stays face down in the middle as the stock-pile. Each player holds his cards concealed in his hand. Whoever has the highest possible number of points (i.e., the double six) begins and lays this card in the middle of the table. If the double six happens to be in the stock-pile you can begin with the double five. The next player's card must match the previous one either in terms of number, color, number of images or shape. You may lay on at either end. Cards with double numbers should be laid crosswise. Each player may lay on several cards, provided they fit. If a player has no card in his hand that matches the cards already on the table he can either buy from the stock-pile or miss out a turn, if there are no cards left. The game is finished when one player has laid out all his cards. The other players may continue playing if they wish, the loser being the one who has the largest number of cards or points at the end.

Dominoes as a dice game. You need 28 domino cards with points or numbers, and two dice. Any number of people may play. Lay the cards face upwards on the table, except the double zero card. Arrange the others either chronologically from $\frac{1}{0}$ to $\frac{6}{0}$ or else mixed up

arbitrarily, whichever is more difficult. Cast the dice for the cards from $\frac{1}{0}$ to $\frac{6}{0}$. A player may take the card that corresponds to the number he has thrown on the dice. Hence if he throws a 3, he may take the card with $\frac{3}{0}$; or if he throws a 6, he may take the $\frac{6}{0}$, and so on. If the relevant card has already been taken, then he must pass the turn. Once the cards from $\frac{1}{0}$ to $\frac{6}{0}$ have been cast for in this way, the game continues with two dice. For example, if a player throws a 4 and a 2, he

takes the card with $\frac{4}{2}$. He can continue throwing until there are no cards left corresponding to the number of points on the dice. *What to do:* Take a strip of cardboard 28 cm × 2 cm (11″ × $\frac{3}{4}$″). Then take an office punch and punch dots out of a sheet of black self-adhesive foil. If you are making the game for children you can use six different colors. For example, blue for 1, yellow for 2, black for 3, red for 4, green for 5, and violet for 6. Glue the dots onto the cards

following the pattern of the dominoes illustrated on pages 110 and 113 and then you are ready to cut the cards out. Cover the matchbox with black and the slide with yellow adhesive foil. Cut a narrow strip of yellow foil, 2 mm ($\frac{1}{16}$″) wide and about 10 cm (4″) long, and glue it down the middle of the matchbox. Then glue the dots either side of it according to the layout of a domino card.

Parents nowadays often start children's play groups or kindergartens. It is very expensive to buy all the necessary games in large numbers. But if you work in a team or in the family circle, you will find you can make many of these games yourselves.

Page 113 shows a simple idea which children can easily copy. For the number six you make a bunch of six grapes consisting of six white dots glued on and colored with soft-tipped pens. Children can also draw and paint the designs for suns, cherries, fir-trees, houses and fishes.

The illustration on page 113 shows some possibilities for laying the cards on the board. The dotted lines are only included to simplify it for you. They should not appear on the final work. For the matchbox, trace the motif, transfer it onto self-adhesive foil, cut it out and stick one motif on either side of the sample card. Stick one of the motifs in white or blue on the top of the matchboxes. The pieces can be stored in matchboxes or cigarette boxes. They also come in useful as small presents.

Animal jigsaw puzzles. The animals shown here consist of three equal parts which fit neatly into a suitable packet. *You will need:* seven pieces of cardboard measuring 7.5 sq. cm (3 sq. in.), a black ball-point pen, colored soft-tipped pens and self-adhesive transparent foil.

What to do: Trace the outline of the animals and the blue dividing lines onto transparent paper, such as grease-proof paper. Then transfer it onto both sides of the piece of cardboard, using carbon paper. Color the animals brightly using fiber-tipped pens and cover up the outline tracing with ball-point pen or water color. Cover the square cards with transparent foil and cut along the blue dividing lines so that each animal separates into three parts. *How to play:* 1. Lay the pieces of the animals together again. 2. Jumble up the various sections of the different animals so that you create new, very amusing animal configurations, for example two-headed beasts or birds with an elephant's foot and the tail of a fish.

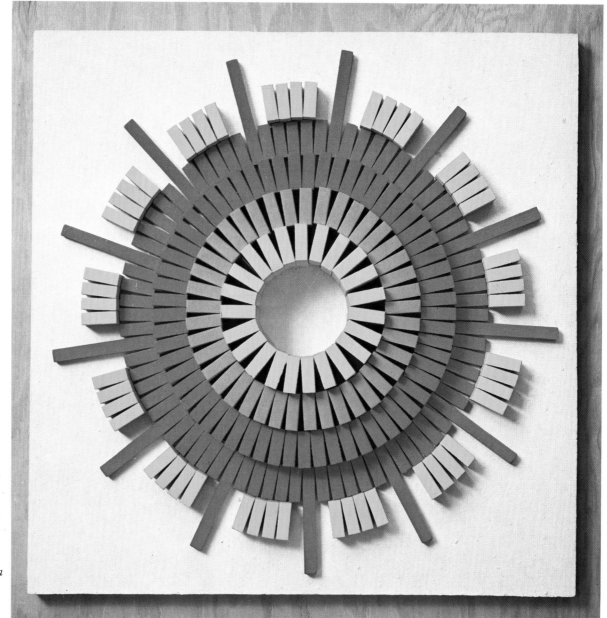

This sketch of the cross-section of the "Sun" motif will give you an idea of its construction. As in the case of the "Sun" motif, start by cutting your wooden blocks in the desired lengths. Here we used 2 cm, 1.8 cm, 1.6 cm, 1.4 cm, 1.2 cm ($\frac{3}{4}$, $\frac{11}{16}$, $\frac{5}{8}$, $\frac{9}{16}$, $\frac{1}{2}$″).

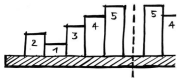

The decorative effect comes from a successful combination of bright colors and otherwise plain and even monotonous shapes.

Wall decorations

These decorations are bright and imaginative forms made from cheap, easily obtainable materials. You can use them for the walls of your living room or hall, or anywhere else in your house, school or club.

Painted parquet blocks: Making wall decorations by arranging, layering, shifting, juxtaposing and fanning out parquet blocks is almost like playing with children's blocks. The oak parquet blocks used for the step-board and sun patterns measure 13.8 cm ×

All the objects here, some of them described very briefly and accompanied by only one illustration, are intended as suggestions. Don't just copy the processes. Use them as a basis for experimentation.

3 cm × 0.8 cm ($5\frac{1}{2}''$ × $1\frac{1}{4}''$ × $\frac{3}{8}''$). You don't have to buy top-quality blocks; seconds will do. Alternatively, you can substitute parquet blocks with thin planed laths or pieces of square plank cut to the appropriate size. The colorful "Stepboard" is designed to brighten a fairly small, dull wall space and measures 25 cm × 17 cm ($10''$ × $6\frac{3}{4}''$). Having polished the blocks, select a particular shade of color for each one. Starting at the bottom of the board, build up your step design row by row. The second row is identical to the first, except that you should

side view

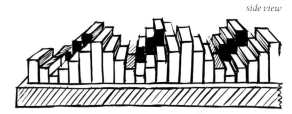

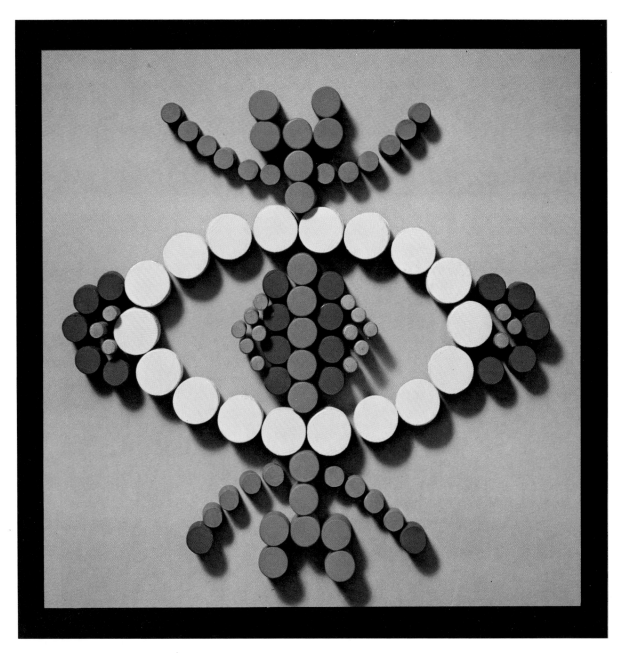

The corks and rounds of wood are not glued directly onto the base. As you can see in the sectional sketch, the pieces of stiff wire are inserted into corks and wooden rounds. The ends of the wire are filed to a point. Stick the "dots" as deep as you like into the polystyrene base (5 cm thick – 2"). If you are only using corks, toothpicks will do instead of wire.

arrange your colors in a different order. The third is an exact repeat of the first. And so on.

For the "Sun" motif, saw the wood blocks into lengths varying between 1 and 5 cm ($\frac{3}{8}$" × 2"), using a miter block. For the base you will need a board measuring 40 cm² (16" × 16") which you paint white. Instead of using a compass, arrange the central ring of wood blocks round a small soup can or tin. This inner ring should be 5 cm (2") high. Any glue will do to stick the pieces onto the base. When you have finished your

design, you can add a simple frame round the edge of the board. Finally, give the whole work a coat of colorless varnish.

Making patterns out of corks and rounds of wood. Young people in particular are always ready to change the furnishing and decoration of their rooms. The wall decoration shown here is very suitable for this as it can easily be re-arranged, re-painted and re-hung. It consists of rounds of wood from the handicraft shop cut in various sizes and smoothed off with sand-paper. You can also use large bottle corks. To ensure that your pattern is clear, stick to one size for either the rounds of wood or the corks. Limit yourself to one color for pieces of the same size. Corks or rounds of wood of the same size and color should be arranged evenly over the surface in order to maintain the balance of the composition. As a base, use a piece of polystyrene 5 cm (2″) thick, covered with some fairly lightweight material such as jute or grass-

ranging from those used for drinks, pharmaceutical products and cosmetics, to spices, inks and chemical products.

The decoration illustrated here was inspired by no-return beer bottles. Try it yourself with different types of bottles. By experimenting in this way you will come across new ideas. The shapes of the bottles are not particularly striking in themselves. However, if you put two bottles top to top

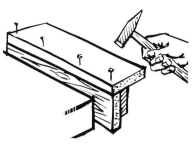

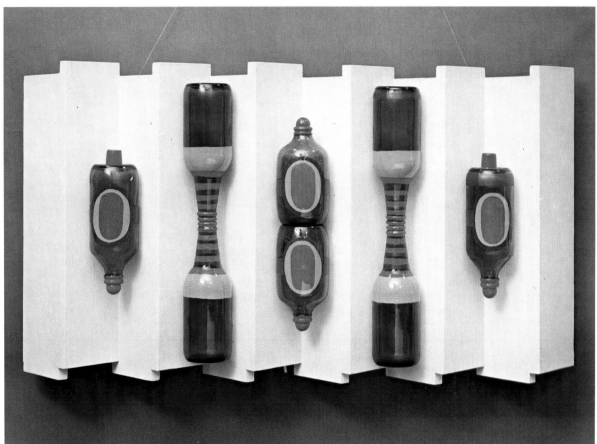

Glue the eight bottles to the zigzag wall with an all-purpose glue. The wall consists of 12 plywood planks 1.5 cm ($\frac{5}{8}$″) thick and 12 cm ($4\frac{3}{4}$″) long. To join them, screw one plank into the planing machine so that you can nail the second one to it at right angles. It is a good idea to remove the heads of the nails with a hammer. The sketch above shows the planks joined together to make a flat row. Below, you can see how they are set at an angle to form the zigzag wall.

For this kind of work use not only objects you make yourself out of wood or clay, but ready-made things, such as bottles.

cloth which you can dye yourself if you wish. It is advisable to use a synthetic cold glue. The corks and rounds of wood should be between 6 and 35 mm ($\frac{1}{4}$″ and $1\frac{1}{2}$″) in diameter. diameter.

Bottles: Bottles can be adapted to different uses, as you can see from the illustration. In this case they are not used for storing liquids, nor even as vases. Emphasis is laid instead on the purely visual effects of the different shapes. The idea of mounting painted bottles on a board exploits the countless different shapes and sizes of bottles in daily use,

or bottom to bottom they no longer look like mere bottles, but assume an entirely new dimension. Whether you join them at the tops or the bottoms, the formal effect is quite different – especially when you think of the whole as though it consists of a single piece rather than of two separate bottles.

In the pendant bottle decoration this transformation is emphasized still more by adding touches of color, for example red rings, to the bottle ends. You can transform the bottles even more dramatically by adding red glass balls and by placing a red cork on the base, suggesting the presence of another opening. But you do not have to decorate your bottles by painting them (if you do, use synthetic resinous paint). Try using the various shades of brown, green and colorless bottles currently available, arranging them to make an interesting pattern.

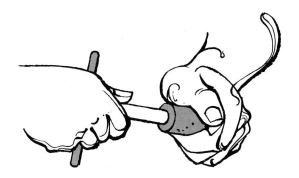

wrong   right

Puppet heads: These are the heads of a set of puppets which was never finished. You can follow the design and make a most unusual mural for a bed-sitter or a school or drama club-room. The puppets' heads – all sixteen of them (although you can reduce or increase the number) are made from modelling clay in one of the brands obtainable from art materials suppliers. Follow the maker's instructions in each case. You may have to mix a powder with water, but some modelling clay is produced ready for moulding from the plastic bag or tub which keeps it moist. When you have moulded the heads you fix them to a *papier mâché* base of the required size, leave to dry for three to four days (according to the instructions on the package), and then paint with poster colors. Of course it's preferable to paint the heads before sticking them to the board, for that will allow you to get at all the difficult parts. Later on you can cover the whole thing with clear varnish. Then it can be framed as you wish.

Materials

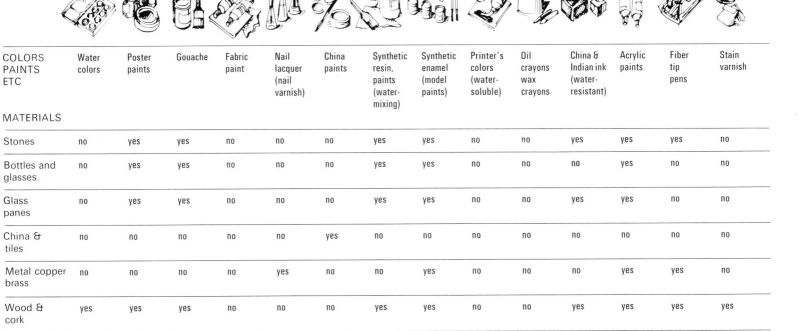

COLORS PAINTS ETC MATERIALS	Water colors	Poster paints	Gouache	Fabric paint	Nail lacquer (nail varnish)	China paints	Synthetic resin, paints (water-mixing)	Synthetic enamel (model paints)	Printer's colors (water-soluble)	Oil crayons wax crayons	China & Indian ink (water-resistant)	Acrylic paints	Fiber tip pens	Stain varnish
Stones	no	yes	yes	no	no	no	yes	yes	no	no	yes	yes	yes	no
Bottles and glasses	no	yes	yes	no	no	no	yes	yes	no	no	no	yes	no	no
Glass panes	no	yes	yes	no	no	no	yes	yes	no	no	yes	yes	no	no
China & tiles	no	no	no	no	no	yes	no	no	no	no	no	no	no	no
Metal copper brass	no	no	no	no	yes	no	no	yes	no	no	no	yes	yes	no
Wood & cork	yes	yes	yes	no	no	no	yes	yes	no	no	yes	yes	yes	yes
Paper cardboard papier mâché	yes	yes	yes	no	no	no	yes	no	yes	yes	yes	yes	yes	no
Lino-cuts fabric-printing	no	no	no	yes	no	no	no	no	yes	no	no	no	no	no
Eggs	yes	yes	yes	no	no	no	yes	no	yes	yes	yes	yes	yes	no
Undercoat/ primer	yes	yes	yes	—	—	—	—	with wood: yes	—	—	—	—	—	—
Thinner	water	water	water	water	acetone	special purpose thinner	water	special purpose thinner	water	turpen-tine	—	water	—	—
Lacquer	colorless varnish	colorless varnish or wax	colorless varnish	—	—	—	colorless varnish	—	—	varnish	colorless varnish	varnish	varnish	colorless varnish

PLEASE NOTE: This tabular summary is intended only as a rough guide to possibilities. Always follow the instructions and warnings accompanying materials and colors, and whenever possible consult your crafts supplier, art materials dealer and other experts. This is especially important in the case of solvents or thinners and lacquers or varnishes. The composition of materials and paints varies from country to country, and maker to maker. Always try out colors and materials, and all mixtures and solutions, before beginning work.

Color guide

On passing through a glass prism, white light emerges as the various colors of the solar spectrum. This color scale (violet, blue, green, yellow, orange, red) can be arranged in the form of a color circle divided into twelve equal parts, which we reproduce here as a multi-colored "flower".

The three neutral primary or basic colors *yellow* (cadmium yellow 1), *red* (magenta 5) and *blue* (cyan blue 9) lie at the three angles of an imaginary equilateral triangle. Opposite each of these are the "first-order" secondary colors: violet (7), medium green (11), orange (3). These are formed from 50% each of two basic colors. All pairs of diametrically opposed colors are known as "complementary colors".

For example: violet (7) mixed from 50% magenta (5) and 50% light blue (9) is the complementary color to cadmium yellow (1). Between the three basic colors and their three secondary colors come their intermediate shades or tones ("second-order" secondary colors): 2, 4, 6, 8, 10, 12.

If you want to go further than these "pure" colors you can mix in a little of the complementary color.

By lightening the colors with white or mixing in very small amounts of black you get more variations which go just as well together.

The eye sees the "reddest", or most intense, red as nearer to yellow than on the color circle shown here. The cold magenta (5) has to be used for technical printing reasons, whereas when actually mixing colors you use carmine (4) as a basic color.

It's most important to mix colors using the same thinner. In other words, don't mix watercolors and enamel paints.

Don't forget to use freshly rinsed brushes for each of the colors you choose. And remember that this chart is only a rough guide: colors will vary considerably from country to country, and supplier to supplier.

1 cadmium yellow
2 orange
3 scarlet
4 carmine
5 magenta
6 purple
7 violet
8 ultramarine
9 light blue
10 turquoise (cyan)
11 medium-green
12 yellow-green

123

Acknowledgments

Some of the photographs, drawings and in a few cases texts in this volume appeared originally in books published in the Leisure Crafts series by Search Press, London, Great Britain.

The photographs are by Toni Schneiders. The objects, texts and drawings are by the following:

Doris Epple
M.-S. Erhart
Margrit Kubiak-
  Winkelmann
Brigitte Gicklhorn-
  Pramer
Hedwig and Benno
  Kretzschmar-Volck
K. Bree
A. Scherer
S. Speck
W. Kuttler
B. Naumann
Eleonore Hüni
W. Kretzer
Werner Roll

Agnes Gaensslen
U. Schneiders
H. Gaensslen
Margret Kiene
A. Kutschera
Hermine Skomal
Elisabeth Hammer
Helene Hornumg
Herbert Becker
H. Lüthi
N. and J. Friedrich
H. Haupt-Battaglia
Hans Fasold
D. Weinmann
Gerhard Frank

Index